INTERNATIONAL FAIRS

Also by Nigel Heard—

Wool: East Anglia's Golden Fleece

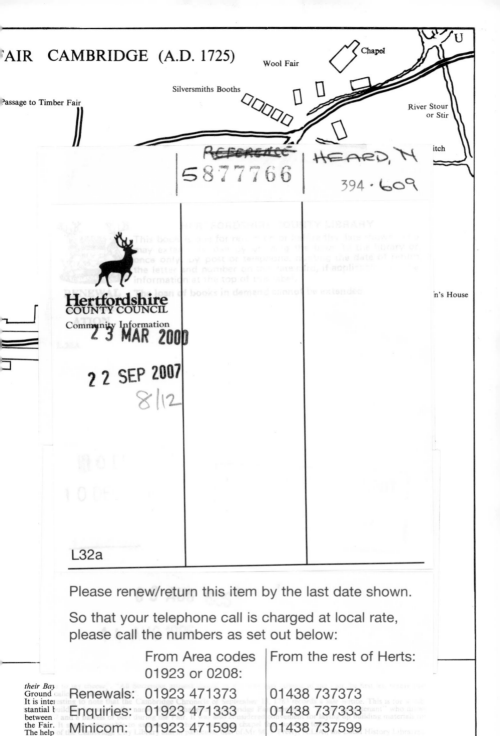

AIR CAMBRIDGE (A.D. 1725)

Wool Fair

Chapel

Silversmiths Booths

Passage to Timber Fair

River Stour
or Stir

itch

n's House

their Bay
Ground
It is interesting to note
stantial b
between
the Fair.
The help
and his s

INTERNATIONAL FAIRS

by

NIGEL HEARD Ph.D.

Lecturer in History at
Lady Spencer-Churchill
College of Education, Oxford.

TERENCE DALTON LIMITED
LAVENHAM   .   SUFFOLK
1973

Published by
TERENCE DALTON LIMITED
SBN 900963 37 9

Printed in Great Britain at
The Lavenham Press Limited
Lavenham   Suffolk

Contents

Index of Illustrations

Illustrations acknowledged *Old England* are from *Old England: A Pictorial Museum of Regal, Ecclesiastical, Municipal, Baronial and Popular Antiquities,* by Charles Knight, published by James Sangster, London.

To My Parents.

Introduction

ALTHOUGH the medieval fair may seem remote from modern times, a relic of a bygone age, in many ways the situation of the modern Western World is very similar to that in the Middle Ages. Such a consideration makes the study of the underlying influences that created the fair much more than a mere reappraisal of an interesting link with the past. The modern fair plays only a very minor role in today's society, no longer fulfilling an essential function in the national economy. What fundamental changes have taken place in our civilisation to have relegated the fair from its former position of importance? This question will be answered to a certain extent in the unfolding story of the fair, but much of the enigma can only explained in the basic economic changes in the world. Twentieth century Europeans, long accustomed to holding an economic and political pre-eminence in the world, tend to forget that for a greater part of man's existence Europe was an insignificant backwater surrounded by nations of greater strength and wealth. In the pages of history, European supremacy is of very recent origin, and is already beginning to wane: a circumstance which makes the story of the fair very applicable.

Man has created some form of civilised life for himself for seven thousand years, but it is only during the last three centuries that Europe has had world wide dominance. Indeed except for the comparatively brief period of the Roman Empire the West was extremely backward in comparison with many other parts of the world. The great centres of civilisation were the Near East, India, and China, whereas for some four thousand years, Europe was only an underdeveloped area on the fringe of the Mediterranean. The one point of contact was through trade, Levantine merchants coming to the West in search of metals, especially tin and copper. With the growth of Greek civilisation the spread of trade and population led to the establishment of colonies in Italy, France and Spain. This acted in the same manner as European colonisation in Africa in the nineteenth century, and brought a thin veneer of culture to the West. Until the emergence of the Romans as a

8

military power in the last centuries of the pre-christian era, Europe remained primitive. With the growth of the Roman Republic, and the expansion of the Empire into the Near East, Europe's problem of a chronic shortage of natural bullion supplies was overcome, as the gold and silver mines of the Levant fell into Western control. The Roman Empire circling the Mediterranean, commanded the greater part of the world's trade, and had links with Far Eastern commerce through the overland route to India and China. Europe became wealthy as trade prospered under the influence of the 'pax romana', and vast quantities of bullion flowed into the West. After four hundred years, however, the might of Rome began to dwindle, and the pressure of the barbarian hordes built up along the Rhine and Danube frontiers. Already the Empire had been divided into Eastern and Western sections, and it was the Byzantine Empire based upon Constantinople that continued to expand.

During the fifth century Western Europe fell to the German tribesmen, and well before then great numbers of Roman nobles and merchants had fled to Greece taking their wealth with them. The West was systematically plundered, quantities of treasure being hidden and never recovered and even more was lost, or squandered. This was the beginning of the Dark Ages, which lasted for the next five hundred years. The West was no longer part of a strong trading area, and denuded of her wealth she had no means of replenishing it. Possessing no rich natural sources of bullion, trade was the only means of acquiring gold and silver. Although tenuous links were maintained with the Byzantine Empire until the seventh century, these were broken by the Arab naval victories that gave them the control of the Mediterranean. Even Spain, which had the largest mineral mines then worked, was overrun by the Moslems. Europe was thrown back on her own resources, and a grim period of austerity followed, when the farming communities had to struggle for self-sufficiency. It was during this time that the countries of the West formed themselves into a loose economic federation through the feudal society; the age which saw the rebirth of the fair. Economic necessity transcended national frontiers, and the incessant wars, in the struggle for survival. Although divided into a number of warring nations, Europe became an international unit within which there were no commercial frontiers. Social barriers were horizontal, but all over Europe men of the same class could mix without any difficulty. Within this society the fair and the market became the means of maintaining an even flow of Europe's natural assets.

By the eleventh century Europe, although still economically and culturally backward, had built up a stronger military organisation. Efforts were made to break out of the isolation which had separated the West from the more advanced civilisations of the Near and the Far East. The Crusades were both a religious and military reaction against the Moslem empires, and, although having only limited military success, they did re-establish contact with the Levant. A fragile commercial link was maintained with Palestine through the city states of Italy. Along this route came a meagre trickle of trade which very slowly replenished the European bullion supplies, and allowed a gradual expansion in the economy. Very slowly a new and vigorous medieval civilisation was created, which, although hampered by constant wars and narrow prejudice, was to overshadow the great powers under whose shadow Europe had existed for so long.

The great Western expansion of the fifteenth century was motivated by commercial necessity. The rise of the powerful Ottoman Empire in the Levant during the fourteenth century threatened the West's slender link with Palestine and the overland route to the Far East. The fall of Constantinople in 1453 only underlined the impending danger. This led to a drive to find an alternative route to the Indies, and the all important spice trade. Pioneered by Portuguese and Spanish explorers, new eastern and western routes were opened up to India and China. Suddenly the whole Western outlook had undergone a dramatic change. The Mediterranean ceased to be the centre of the world, the oceans providing the gateway to a greater destiny. At the same time Western society no longer depended upon self-sufficiency, and the need for international economic co-operation had vanished. The new doctrine of nationalism became established as the countries of Europe vied to take advantage of the commercial prospects opening up in the New World. Western seapower and technology in firearms gave her a decided superiority over the older and richer nations of the Far East. The old spirit of interdependence had gone, as now the vast overseas markets gave scope for all. The economic unity disappeared in a drive to establish colonial and commercial empires, which in turn convulsed Europe in a series of colonial and trade wars. Monopolies and tariffs appeared as each nation attempted to preserve dominions, and prevent other countries from gaining a world supremacy. During the eighteenth century Britain underwent an industrial and agricultural revolution, and won supremacy in the colonial struggle. In the early decades of the nineteenth century Britain led the world, but by the end of the century her lead was being overtaken.

Other European nations, notably Germany, had adopted, and improved upon, British industrial methods, and came to claim a share in the world markets. More significantly former under-developed colonial areas, such as the United States, were becoming industrialised, and they too began to compete against the European nations. Rapid technological advances soon began to neutralise the initial industrial advantages of the Western nations. The First World War did much to resolve the situation in favour of the newer countries. The Depression of the Thirties was an eloquent testimonial to the blockage in world markets. This, followed almost immediately by the Second World War, com-pleted the discomforture of the European countries. A war-devastated Europe awoke in the Forties to a new and hostile commercial situation, in which she no longer held a premier position. The two super-powers, the United States of America and Russia, possessed resources and power beside which Europe paled into insignificance. The development of China, and the emergence of Japan as a leading commercial competitor made the picture even more bleak. The Continental countries, building up their war-shattered economies, were quicker to appreciate the new situation. Britain was slower to adjust, especially as she was undergoing the trauma of giving independence to the remainder of her empire. A new spirit of co-operation appeared on the Continent, born of the need to compete against the great powers of East and West, the result of which was the creation of the Common Market.

Thus the wheel has come full cycle with a return to the economic conditions of the Middle Ages, when a puny Europe had to struggle against the might of the great civilisations. Today the menace from East is not the Moslem hordes, but the mechanised might of Russia, with ever enigmatical China hovering in the back-ground. The protective bastion of Constantinople has been replaced by the strike power of the United States of America, but still Europe nestles between the contending strength of greater nations. As in the medieval period Europe lacks the natural resources to compete individually on equal terms with larger countries of the world. To survive, trade is essential, without a return to the now impossible doctrine of self-sufficiency. Formerly Britain formed an integral and vital part of the European trading zone, and out of this grew her economic strength. In the unfavourable conditions of world trade can Britain afford not to form part of the new European trading area? The Common Market from the historical point of view might well take the place of the fair cycle, which once rejuvenated Western Europe.

I

Ancient Fairs

TODAY the fair is rapidly disappearing, and the fairgrounds are being swallowed up, as our ever-growing population and towns spread into the countryside. The showmen and barkers are a vanishing breed because their camping sites are being closed down, and they have, unwillingly, to conform to the twentieth century. The day of the fair has passed, and it has been finally sacrificed to the modern god of television. Yet this is only part of the story, because the fair had been losing its place in society for several hundred years. Its original religious significance gone, the fair had become important as a centre of exchange, but when new ways of trade were found the fair could not secure a lasting rôle in society. No longer a bustling centre of commerce the fairground continued to be a major place of entertainment: then with the coming of the railways in the nineteenth century travel became much easier, and people had less need of amusement on the village green. Since then the cinema, the motor car and television have come to provide more sophisticated enjoyment.

The fair has a very long and honourable history which dates back many thousands of years, and is as old as trade itself. When during the Stone Ages man overcame the basic needs of survival in the struggle against his environment, the first ideas of trade began to emerge: and so the simple principle of barter between individuals and tribes was well established in Western Europe before the beginning of the Bronze Age. Life was very primitive, and even the simplest type of trade was difficult. The population of the whole Continent of Europe was only a few millions, and these tribes were widely separated by dense forest mountains and swamps. With their light and rudimentary tools these people could farm only the lightest and poorest soils, and made little impression on clearing the wilderness surrounding them. Travel and communications were extremely difficult except along the rivers, or across the upland ridges that rose above the prevalent forest and marsh. These spines of chalk and limestone were widely used by those wishing to travel, and became well-beaten trackways criss-crossing Western Europe.

Until the time of the Roman Empire the whole of Western Europe, except for the lands immediately bordering the Mediterranean, remained relatively backward. At the same time, however, the countries around the eastern end of the Mediterranean were much more advanced. The Egyptians, Phoenicians and Greeks developed great civilisations based upon town life. With the discovery of the use of bronze, there was an immediate and growing demand for the tin and copper from which it was made. The hitherto remote and barbaric lands of Western Europe now became more important as a possible source of these metals. Travellers and merchants, especially the Phoenicians, began to visit these distant lands. Gradually the fabled island of Britain, home of the North Wind, became known as the Tin Island, famous for its legendary wealth. After several centuries metal tools began to be used more widely in Western Europe. Wandering smiths and pedlars braved the dangers of these wild, and often hostile, lands in the search for trade. They followed the system of trackways, their progress being marked by lonely graves and burial mounds. These pioneers were the heralds of more advanced tribesmen using bronze, and later iron tools and weapons, who conquered the fertile lowland areas of Europe, and drove the less civilised peoples into highland zones.

These peoples were more civilised, and contacts with the lands around the Mediterranean became stronger as trade became more important. The highly civilised nations of the Near East with their large urban populations needed the metals, foodstuffs and raw materials of Western Europe. In return they traded jewellery, silk, tools and other luxuries unobtainable in the West. The essential link between Europe and the eastern Mediterranean world was Italy. Merchants from the Greek colonies in Sicily and southern Italy crossed the Alpine passes, and then followed the course of the river Rhine until they reached the North Sea. From the mouth of the Rhine it was easy to reach Britain and the lands around the Baltic. Four thousand years ago a pattern of trade was in the process of creation which was to serve Europe for many centuries, and was only destroyed by the maritime upheavals of the fifteenth century. It was a pattern woven by the nomad and the itinerant pedlar wending his way past half-forgotten landmarks to an uncertain destination.

These tramping, dusty feet carved out paths and trackways which were to be used by unknown generations when their original purpose was forgotten. A way of life was being wrought out of the seasons and the needs of a primitive mankind living close to the land. Like the seasons this mode of exchange became a virtually unchangeable annual round, which became mellowed by the passage of time. The sporadic invasions of Bronze and Iron Age tribes only strengthened the pattern. Not even the growth of the mighty Roman Empire brought noticeable changes, only augmenting the avenues of trade through the network of roads that the legions spread across the face of Europe. The magic and the lure of the road could only disappear when the needs out of which it was born ceased to exist, and new needs brought a fresh way of life.

From these early stirrings of trade, catering for the basic requirements of humanity, the fair was to develop. Apart from the centuries when Europe was ruled from Rome there was little change in the condition of society until the coming of the Renaissance. A mankind that was only just winning the battle against nature, and was always faced with the dangers of famine, plague and flood. A small population of farmers scratching a bare living out of the unwilling soil, but men aware of their own destiny, and battling to improve their uneventful lot. To them the pedlar and travelling merchants were a welcome break in the monotony of the normal round, providing them with a glimpse of the outside world, albeit at second-hand. It was from the pedlars that the country people could buy the trinkets, tools and weapons that they could not make for themselves. In this way new ideas and inventions found their way slowly into the remotest corners of the continent. Over the centuries certain places and times were singled out for these exchanges which had begun as casual meetings. These sites were chosen for their convenience, and were placed in, or near, the largest villages along the most used trackways. Frequently this was impossible because many villages were situated away from the trackways, so that the meetings were held near to some prominent landmark, a hill, a burial mound, or one of the great figures carved out of the chalk downs. Naturally for people living close to nature the times for such meetings had to be chosen to blend in with the seasons. The winter months were ignored because bad weather made it too difficult to travel, whilst in the spring the farmers were preoccupied with sowing their crops. The summer months and the early autumn period after the harvest were obviously times when people had some leisure, and, of equal importance, there were surplus goods to barter in exchange for the merchandise of the pedlars.

The choice of sites for these ancient fairs was deeply influenced by religion. In an unsophisticated society religion was an essential part of nature, to be seen in sky, rivers and wind, forces that had to be placated if man was to survive. The miracles of the rising sun, and the rebirth of the world in the spring were to be wondered at, and appeased by sacrifice. The gods were everywhere and had to be worshipped with due solemnity. Chief among them was the sun, and the solstices were marked with special ceremonies, particularly the 22nd June, Midsummer Day. Similarly sowing and harvest times had their own festivals, the spring fertility rites to ensure the growth of the crops, and the thanksgiving to celebrate when the crops were safely harvested for the year. Such occasions were ideal for the itinerant trader as there were likely to be large gatherings of people in holiday mood, who were likely to buy his goods. The pedlars and merchandise they had to offer were welcomed as part of the festivals. Merchants, in consequence, carefully arranged their routes and times of travel to coincide with those gatherings that were accessible to the trackways. In this manner religious meetings became great social events of the year, to be discussed until the allotted time came round again. Wild pagan ceremonies and rites in the early dawn, followed by sports and feasting intermingled with a melee of buying and selling lasting well into the night.

The arrival of the Romans temporarily removed much of the dangerous glamour of the road as much of Western Europe was sheltered under the cloak of the 'pax romana'. Life became strictly ordered under the direction of army officers and tax collectors. Religious life became restricted and channelled into the official beliefs of the Empire despite the liberal attitude of the Romans towards native theologies. Moreover, towards the end of the Empire in the West, Christianity was adopted as the state religion, and pagan rites were assiduously repressed. The itinerant trade suffered from the economic strength of the Romans. The wealth of the world flowed through the Empire, making it easy for the local tribesmen to buy foreign goods at the nearest town without the need for the pedlar. It seemed as though the ancient fair was doomed, yet it was from the Romans that the fair was to get its name.

The Romans worshipped a great number of gods. Each individual had his own special god, and many of the gods had their own particular festive days, marked by set ceremonies. These occasions were called 'feria', a holiday, and gradually the term was extended to include similar meetings and truces all over the Empire. Beyond the frontiers of the Roman world lay the territories and kingdoms of the barbarians who were constantly resisting and pressing against the might of the Empire. The main contact with these lands was through commerce, encouraged by the powerful financial interests of the City. Enterprising merchants visited these territories and established the first communications. Then on some pretext the Roman legions marched in to conquer the country. They were followed by the financiers and contractors, who reaped the profits. For this reason trade was encouraged along all the frontiers. Local commanders would make temporary truces to allow trading between the frontier towns and the tribesmen, and in due course this occasion became known as a 'feria'. During the four hundred years that the Romans occupied Britain these meetings became quite frequent, especially along the line of Hadrian's Wall.

This may seem to be very remote from modern times, or, indeed, from the great medieval fairs, but a pattern of trade was being created from which the famous international fairs were to develop. The traditional trackways and meeting places became so deeply etched in men's minds that only the change from Mediterranean to maritime trade brought them into disuse. During the fifth century the falling birth-rate, and declining economy of the western part of the Roman Empire enabled the barbarians to break through the frontiers, and overrun the lands to the west of the Rhine. The new settlers were uncivilised farmers who had little conception of the Roman way of life. Although the barbarian kingdoms, helped by the Catholic Church, tried to emulate the Roman methods of government, romanisation gradually died away. A new pattern of settlement and an entirely different society emerged that was based upon the village, not the town. Gone was the peace and order of the 'pax romana', towns and roads fell into disrepair. Western Europe had returned to the conditions that had reigned before the advent of the Romans and the old ways of communication reasserted themselves. Ancient trackways assumed a renewed importance, and traditional meeting places came back into use. Most of the great medieval towns and industrial centres grew out of the Roman towns, or villages sited along the trackways, or a Roman road. This was because the medieval earth roads were virtually unuseable for much of the year which meant that fairs were frequently sited on the Prehistoric meeting places. Two of the greatest of the English fairs can trace their origin in this way. St Giles' Fair,

Winchester, one of the largest of the early fairs, was held under the shadow of Long Barrow, a landmark and meeting place for thousands of years. Here is a classical example of a town and fair developing out of Prehistoric and Roman origins. Stourbridge Fair, Cambridgeshire, although of a much later date owed much of its importance to its proximity to the ancient trackway of the Icknield Way, and claimed to have its origins in Roman times.

It is true, of course, that only a fraction of the medieval fairs owed their direct origin in this way. The steady growth of population, and the new patterns of settlement had a considerable effect upon the structure of Europe. Yet even in many cases where there appears to be no direct connection at first sight, Pre-history has played its part. Before the decrees of the Emperor Constantine established Christianity as the official religion throughout the Roman Empire, the whole of Europe had been pagan for thousands of years. To the great majority of people, grown accustomed to a stream of different religions, the change to Christianity had relatively little effect upon their lives. The Roman Empire had been under increasing pressure from the barbarians hovering along the frontiers, and when the barbarians overran the West Christianity appeared in danger of extinction. The influence and organisation of the Catholic Church enabled it to win the allegiance of the barbarians, and Christianity was accepted in most of the Western countries. No sooner had this been achieved than the Vikings, fierce pagan warriors from the wild, northern lands of Scandinavia, appeared to shatter the newly-one peace. Once again it seemed as though much of the West would revert to paganism, as the Vikings hated Christianity and destroyed churches and monasteries. Gradually the Vikings settled down on the lands which they had won, and were converted to Christianity. This marked the last major crisis of the Church in its battle against paganism, but Christianity had only a tenuous hold.

Clearly paganism had deep roots in Europe and its peoples, especially as only a tiny minority of Europeans were sufficiently educated to understand what was meant by Christianity. The Church had a stupendous task in combating superstition and witchcraft which had become interwoven into the beliefs of the people, and often had to make concessions to pagan ideas and customs. This was particularly true of festivals such as Yule, when the twelve darkest days of the year were celebrated with feasting as the death of the old year.* The Church identified this with Christmas, and the twelve days of the festival. In the same manner many smaller cult festivals had a similar cloak of respectability cast over them by association with the feast day of a saint, especially one with connections with the locality of the cult. The rites and ceremonies which accompanied such occasions were toned down into innocent country games and sports. The best example of a transformation of this nature was maypole dancing, which was originally a pagan fertility rite, and became an innocuous country dance. In Prehistoric times these ritual ceremonies were held at well known landmarks and attracted large crowds, which in turn provided a ready market for itinerant merchants. The feast days under the protection of a saint developed along similar lines. At first these fairs were times for people to meet together to enjoy themselves, and it was only later that the traders moved in to exploit the potential sales. In many ways the modern fair with its amusement and funfairs carries on the age-old traditions of our pagan forebears.

---

*During the eighteenth century the changeover from the Julian to the Gregorian calendar caused a change of eleven days which accounts for the difference between our Christmas and those before the eighteenth century.

The Dark Ages

THE DARK Ages in Western Europe began when the western part of the Roman Empire fell to the barbarians, and lasted until the final Viking settlements in the eleventh century. It was during this period that the economic structure of medieval Europe was forged. A twilight time between the great classical civilisations and the emergence of a new European culture, which is still developing today. A period when the puny barbarian kingdoms, living among the ruins of a mighty Roman past, tried to build themselves a new society. Efforts which were always hampered by an instinctive backward glance to a classical heritage which they did not fully understand.

The power of the Roman Empire had been based upon its wealth and high birth-rate which provided men for the legions. While the armies were able to maintain the 'pax romana' trade flourished, bringing gold and silver into Europe. For some two hundred years before its final collapse the West had been weakened by a falling birth-rate, which made it difficult to fend off the barbarian attacks. This had forced the Imperial Government to come to terms with the more romanised barbarians living along the frontiers, who were allowed to settle in depopulated areas within the boundaries of the Empire. In return the settlers were expected to help the Romans to resist the invasions of their less fortunate kinsmen. This situation led to even more contact and trade with the barbarians, and as the two peoples began to integrate there was an increase in the number of local truces. As the power of the central government continued to decline people began to look to the landowners to protect them against the increasing lawlessness. A form of feudalism was developing that was to come to its full fruition during the early part of the Middle Ages. Localism increased as individual areas began to look for their own welfare, and into this came the principle of maintaining trade through the local truce. It was this that the medieval idea of the 'peace of the fair' arose, and was encouraged and augmented by the Church.

The economic stability of the Roman Empire had been based upon a favourable balance of trade, and a sound gold standard currency. As the greater part of the supply of bullion came from outside Europe, the Emperors had to ensure the safety of their eastern and African provinces where the mines were situated. The establishment of a twin capital of Constantinople, and the increasing insecurity in the West led many of the great financiers and nobles to transfer their wealth from Rome to the newer city. By the time of the barbarian invasions Europe was already seriously denuded of gold and silver, and systematic looting further reduced the West to a state of poverty. The situation became even worse when the Vandals, the most rapacious of the invaders, swept through Europe and carried their plunder to Africa to found an empire around the site of ancient Carthage. For a time the Vandals prospered and they built up a powerful pirate fleet which ravaged the western Mediterranean trade routes, effectively cutting off Europe from the Roman Empire in the East. Although the Vandals were eventually crushed by Roman armies from Constantinople the respite did not last very long. During the seventh century a new power arose in Arabia under the influence of the prophet Mohammed, and soon the Moslem armies were sweeping all opposition before them. The Eastern Empire only survived with great difficulty, and within a century Asia Minor and the whole of the north African coast had fallen to Islam. Moslem fleets roved the Mediterranean, and even the greater part of the Visigoth kingdom in Spain had fallen to Moorish invaders. The Pyrenees were crossed and it was only with difficulty that the Moslem invasion of Europe was stopped by the heavily armed Frankish cavalry at the river Loire in 732.

Western Europe was now made up of a group of small semi-barbaric kingdoms, cut off from the civilised lands of the eastern Mediterranean by the fleets of the Barbary corsairs. Trade had come to a virtual stop, and, remote from the centres of culture and commerce, the West began to stagnate. The Germanic tribesmen who now ruled were farmers content to live in scattered groups under their chieftains, who owed only a vague allegiance to the paramount kings. For a time when there was still some contact with the Eastern Empire the kings made token attempts to continue the traditions of Rome. Once this link was severed virtually all traces of effective central government vanished as the kings had neither the knowledge, nor the wealth to establish a strong regime. Town life had broken down and was to continue to decline, while communications steadily worsened. With the collapse of the towns, industry became disrupted, and only continued on a very small scale within the remnants of some of the imperial cities. Life slowly ground to a halt as the machinery of civilisation became choked, and was replaced by feudalism based upon land and military service.

The most noticeable change in Europe at this time was the absence of trade and all the movement and bustle which accompanied it. Commerce is very dependent upon conditions, and the state of the West was unsuitable for any complicated system of international trade. Constant wars between the kingdoms, piracy, and brigandage made it unsafe to travel, and, in any case, the wealthy merchant classes had disappeared, or had been reduced to penury. The chronic shortage of coinage made exchange difficult as most of the available gold and silver had vanished into the coffers of the Church, kings and nobles. Perhaps an even more important factor in this situation was the deteriorating condition of the towns and industries. To the Romans urbanisation had been the key of civilisation, and the whole of the administration had been geared to work through the cities. Even before the final collapse in the West many towns had been declining and becoming depopulated because the people of the countryside had been unable, or unwilling, to support them. Control of the country districts had passed to the great landowners to whom the people looked for leadership and protection. Abandoned by the imperial officials and the administration the towns shrank within their walls until they either disappeared, or became insignificant. During the Dark Ages this situation became much worse, and it was only the presence of the Church that saved them all from complete extinction.

In these chaotic times the Church preserved some state of order, and retained some remnants of Roman civilisation, among a wild and illiterate population. Under the leadership of the Pope, Christendom was organised on the same pattern as the old Empire. Imperial cities, long abandoned by secular officials, remained the centres of ecclesiastical dioceses, and attracted to them whatever remained of the industrial and commercial classes. Here, under the protection of the great cathedrals and monasteries, the first awakening of urban life struggled against the anarchy which surrounded them. These towns were ideally placed to foster the vestiges of trade which persisted in the first part of the Dark Ages. Built on the mighty network of Roman roads, which, apart from the trackways, remained the only effective means of travel until the seventeenth century, they were readily accessible. Even so their existence was precarious, and it was only the later revival of commerce that saved many of them from complete decline.

The true reawakening of Western trade was born not out of the moribund vestiges of the old Empire, but out of the needs of the new society. With the disappearance of a stable financial structure, land had assumed a paramount importance. Wealth and status now depended upon the ownership of land, and a feudal system was evolving in which most payments were made in land and kind. This was an inevitable development in a society where land was plentiful, while gold and silver were at a premium. The people, from king to peasant, were forced to live off the land, and there was scant opportunity for the majority to buy any of the niceties of life. Even the kings could not reside in their own capital towns all the year round because of the difficulties and expense of bringing in sufficient food to support the court. Instead they were forced to travel around their estates, moving from one to the next as the food supplies were exhausted. The peasants were tied to their villages struggling to produce enough to fill their masters' barns, and, if they were fortunate, sufficient to keep themselves alive in the face of the lean winter. It was a drab existence; the main concern was to cling to life despite poor crops, ravaging armies, and the ever-present threat of famine and starvation. Each community became a tightly knit, self-sufficient unit producing the food, clothes, weapons and tools needed by its inhabitants. Small wonder that trade had come to a halt. There was an immense economic recession, yet even among all the drudgery there was the stirrings of a revival.

Slowly some of the scattered tribal villages grew into rambling and untidy towns. This was usually as a result of their position at a crossroads, or at the lowest crossing point of a river. Others became important because of their proximity to a monastery, or a cathedral. As the conditions of the time were so dangerous such towns were defended by ditches and palisades, which made them safer than the surrounding countryside. Moreover the presence of churches and monasteries, although there was always the danger that they might attract rapacious heathen invaders, normally added to the safety and affluence of the inhabitants. Divorced from the crushing, servile regime of village, town dwellers had much greater freedom than the rural population. Within the village the specialist craftsman, such as the blacksmith, had a privileged position because of his essential work, and was freed from many of the servile duties of his fellow peasants. To such men the security and freedom of the towns was a great lure, and many of them escaped from the village to settle in the towns. In this way each town built up a nucleus of craftsmen, and a revival of industry began all over Europe.

The earliest of these urban specialists were the armourers, weapon-smiths, leatherworkers and jewellers. They formed themselves into select communities, and built up a skill far beyond that of the normal village craftsmen. Kings, noblemen and priests who needed, and could afford the goods and workmanship provided by these men, supplied sufficient demand for these embryonic industries to begin to flourish. During the seventh century an increasing number of craftsmen, specialist tradesmen and merchants arrived in the towns, each setting up their own communities within the walls. As the urban populations grew there was an increased demand for food, which enabled the victuallers, such as butchers, bakers, grocers and vintners, to establish communities within the town. By this time the towns were no longer self-contained units, and had to seek supplies from a much wider area. Continued expansion led to greater demands for raw materials and foodstuffs, which encouraged the farmers and landowners to increase their production. As farming prospered, so the country people came in larger numbers to the towns to buy small luxuries which they could not previously afford.

Even without the independent development within the towns the rural communities themselves could not be entirely self-supporting. Certain essential commodities had to be imported from other regions. The most important of these were salt and iron without which the entire routine of the village would have ground to a halt. Without iron the blacksmiths would have been unable to fashion the tools upon which farming depended in its struggle against encroaching nature. Salt, too, was essential for survival. As medieval farmers grew insufficient hay, and virtually no root crops, it was impossible to keep more than a fraction of their livestock through the winter. The remainder had to be salted down after being slaughtered in the autumn, and provided the main supply of meat until the following spring. Iron was obtained from opencast workings, and was crudely smelted in primitive furnaces heated by charcoal. The partially refined iron was set in ingots and distributed by pedlars, who carried the iron on the backs of packhorses. Salt was obtained from easily worked deposits of rock salt, or from evaporation pans on the coast, and was distributed in the same manner. As both these commodities were so valuable they were generally royal monopolies, although the kings usually farmed out the actual marketing to agents. The pedlars engaged in this work were among the first of the true medieval merchants, whose descendents were to become the great merchant princes of later generations.

Herein lay the commercial origin of the medieval fairs. Although feudalism was to be enforced for several more centuries, self-sufficiency proved to be impossible, and some wider method of exchange had to be found. At first such arrangements were very haphazard, and depended more upon chance than organisation. Village communities produced surpluses of wool, hides and foodstuffs to exchange with the pedlars in return for iron and salt. As the population increased larger surpluses could be made, which could be sold elsewhere. Certain areas began to specialise in products suited to their particular region which were exchanged for necessities that they could not provide for themselves. In consequence France and the Rhineland became famed for their wines, while England specialised in wool and grain. Commerce was beginning to move again along the Roman roads and the ancient trackways. Governments were becoming stronger, and society was becoming more peaceful as the influence of Christianity tamed the wilder excesses of the former barbarians. Small markets began to appear in the towns, where the farmers and peasants could exchange their produce for well-made tools, or some small luxuries. As yet, however, trade was on a very small scale, and it was only rarely that people were able to buy goods from overseas.

Western Europe was becoming more settled and there began to be some tentative exchanges between neighbouring kingdoms. Treaties seeking friendship between rival dynasties were usually sealed by a marriage settlement, and an agreement to export, or import certain commodities from each country. Merchants began to travel abroad, and were often rewarded for making a number of overseas voyages. This shows that foreign trade was beginning, but, it must be remembered, that it was unusual enough to merit special notice. Small bands of traders were beginning to travel to foreign countries along the Roman roads and trackways which had virtually fallen into disuse. They joined the native pedlars and merchants who had already begun to distribute the small surpluses from one part of the country to those areas in which they could get the best prices. Occasionally a true 'foreigner' would be found with these groups, a Syrian, or Jewish merchant who had ventured overland from the Levant to sell eastern luxuries in Europe. As this route was so dangerous, few merchants undertook the risk, even for the enormous profits that could be made.

The destination of these travellers were those towns in which industries had begun to revive. It was in the urban centres that the visiting merchant was most likely to be able to sell, or barter, his goods at a reasonable profit. Naturally such merchants would visit those towns with the largest populations, and at times when the most people would be present. Consequently they timed their arrival to coincide with Church festivals and feast days, when they could wait outside the cathedral and sell their goods to the people as they came out. In those days of very slow travel and communication the itinerant merchants soon came to know their routes extremely well. Although their ultimate destination was always the towns they would come to know the points along their routes where they were likely to be able to make sales. Such places were the local religious festivals where the old pagan rites were allowed to continue under the sanction of the Church. Here, too, the merchant would be able to stop, set up makeshift stalls, and sell some of his goods to the merrymakers. Often the traders found it worthwhile to make detours to visit gatherings, and, in time, these fairs would become part of their regular itinerary.

Just as commerce was beginning to make this modest revival new disasters burst upon Western Europe, which were to have a profound effect on the development of trade and the fair. From the north came the longships manned by fierce, heathen Vikings, who looted and traded at will from America in the west to Constantinople in the south east. The viking fleets multiplied rapidly, and for a time it seemed as though England and France would be overrun and become a Viking empire. The threat was overcome, and the Scandinavians settled down in eastern England, northern France and south western Russia. These incursions threw the West into confusion, and prolonged the Dark Ages for another two centuries. Yet out of this chaos emerged a stronger and freer Europe, a Europe in which commerce was to play a much more important part.

Although temporarily weakened by the Viking onslaught, the monarchies, by coping with the danger, were strengthened, and were able to maintain greater peace and security within their domains. The traveller was able to use the roads more freely, safe in the knowledge that some law was being enforced. At the same time the new Scandinavian element in the population introduced a vigorous catalyst in the peoples of Europe. The Vikings were a freedom-loving people who scorned the servile peasantry of the West. Although most of them settled down as farmers, they introduced a new spirit of independence, especially in England. Many of the Vikings did not return to farming, but settled in the towns, attracted by the greater freedom, and the wider possibilities of commerce. It was their arrival which gave a great stimulus to the revival of town life, and greatly increased the numbers of the merchant class.

The town was the key to the situation. The advent of the Vikings changed the status of the town not merely through their own settlement, but, also, because the invasions had altered the royal attitude towards them. The Vikings had won their successes because of their mobility against a static European society. Just in time the kings realised that well fortified and garrisoned towns were a means of slowing down the Scandinavian advance. Roman fortifications were repaired and strengthened, walls and ditches were built, and all over Europe 'burhs' appeared, which gave protection to their inhabitants and to the peasantry living around them.

As early as the seventh century the kings had begun to recognise the importance of trade as a lucrative addition to their revenue. Their difficulty was to find an effective method of collecting taxes from trade when their civil services were small and inefficient. The answer was to limit the places at which trading could take place. Laws were passed laying down the principle that trading should only be carried out in towns before witnesses. This made it much easier for royal officials to collect taxes from the merchants. At the same time it established the essential factor of the fair; all legitimate bargaining had to be carried out before witnesses. The establishment of the 'burhs' gave the town a definite status. They became the centres of trade and were given royal licences, which for a time restricted commerce to these boroughs. Such towns were often given the privilege of minting coins, which, while adding to their importance, ensured that the royal coinage was widely distributed. Here again were developments that were to have fundamental effects upon the growth of the fair. The idea that the right to trade was a royal prerogative, only to be carried out at fixed times and places.

The basis of the great medieval fairs was their royal charter, which was renewed by successive monarchs. The same applied to the more mundane weekly market, which was very important to the routine running of a town. Those towns which received royal licences at this time had a considerable advantage over their rivals that were given this privilege at a later date, and became the great commercial centres of the Middle Ages. Although the charters of most fairs are of a much later date, many claim that they originated from this time despite the lack of documentary evidence. Such arrangements gave the town a position within the feudal world, of which it formed no part and eventually was to replace. As commerce expanded the merchant classes were able to win concessions which made them virtually independent of the feudal lords.

This expansion of trade can be traced directly to the Vikings. To a large extent the military successes of the Vikings was due to their superb seamanship, and the improved design of their longships. Since the fifth century the Germanic tribes had either lost, or never acquired any love of the sea, and this is why Europe had become so hemmed in and cut off from the rest of the world. The Vikings restored the balance, and their daring voyages re-opened the seaways around Europe and into the Mediterranean. Swedish Vikings penetrated the rivers of south western Russia, and, apart from creating a new kingdom, opened up the old trade route from Constantinople to the Baltic. This led to greater contact with the Levant, and eastern luxury goods began to find their way into the West by way of the Baltic. One of the great commercial handicaps had been shortage of coinage, and the Viking wars and the systematic looting of monasteries and churches realised a large amount of gold and silver that had formerly been locked away. This, with the greater initiative of the Scandinavians, gave added impetus to trade. It was not until the eleventh century, however, that commerce was to reassert its full position in Western society.

3   The Pedlars

ALL THESE changes which took place during the six hundred years of the Dark Ages were to have a profound influence upon the medieval fair. This was the formative period when the fraternity of the road came into being, formed of those people who braved the dangers of the road to travel all over Europe. Without these travellers, with their independent outlook, the fairs, and their multifarious activities, would not have been possible.

The men responsible for preserving and expanding trade during the Dark Ages were the handful of itinerant pedlars who continued to travel despite the chaotic conditions. Although they were not hindered by any elaborate system of passports and visas, the position of the trader was very precarious. The absence of any strong governments which could maintain an effective police force meant that the individual was responsible for his own safety. The normal remedy was to seek the collective support of the community in which a person lived. This feudal concept was of little value to the traveller, who, by leaving his community, had virtually put himself outside the protection of feudal law. The greatest protector of the weak, the Church, disapproved of trading as unworthy seeking after riches, and utterly condemned usury. Although this attitude eventually changed, the early merchants could expect little help from ecclesiastical sources. While the pedlar faced constant dangers on the unpoliced roads, he was himself an object of suspicion to those in authority. In an age when all the peasantry was legally bound to the village in which they had been born, men who wandered the roads were extremely conspicuous. It was felt that only nobles, churchmen and royal officials had any right to travel, and that any other wanderers were liable to be brigands, outlaws, or runaway serfs. Consequently the pedlar was quite likely to be arrested, and have his goods confiscated. Apart from this official robbery, the trader set upon by genuine brigands was most unlikely to get any redress from the law.

Another major problem facing the merchant of these times was coinage, in an age when land was the main currency. In the years immediately following the fall of the Empire in the west many of the barbarian kings struggled to maintain the gold standard. The result was ever-increasing monetary chaos, which made the coinage virtually worthless. The situation was somewhat eased by the few contacts with the civilised world which remained to the Europeans. A number of Syrian and Jewish merchants made their way to the West from Asia Minor via the rivers of south west Russia, or through the Balkans. Despite the Arab stranglehold on the Mediterranean there remained one other contact with civilisation through Moslem Spain. The regime in Spain was both civilised and tolerant, and Moorish merchants frequently crossed the Pyrenees to trade with the Europeans. From these sources the West obtained a supply of silks, satins, spices, and a small amount of foreign exchange. As conditions in Western Europe deteriorated the number of these visitors decreased, and by the end of the eighth century contacts with Spain had ceased.

In spite of these conditions there was a certain amount of internal trade. The chronic lack of currency forced the native traders to deal in kind, which was not very convenient. At first the situation was not too difficult because of the presence of the foreign merchants, and the vestiges of currency values. In any case the main internal commerce consisted of the distribution of salt and iron, which was exchanged for the produce from the farms. As the demands of the urban communities increased, however, the need for a simpler method of exchange became necessary. The agents were able to barter in other goods in the course of their journeys, and so carry the goods of one town to sell in the next. This meant that the trader had to carry the goods over a long distance with the danger of breakage, or deterioration. Moreover the pedlar needed to be able to convert his season's trading into hard cash in the autumn so that he could finance his dealings for the next year.

A partial solution came to this problem in the eighth century, when the tottering Merovingian rulers, who controlled most of modern France and Germany, were overthrown. They were replaced by the more vigorous Carolingians, who immediately set about finding a solution to the monetary crisis. Charles the Great was mainly responsible for establishing a form of currency, which continued to be used in England until the conversion to decimal currency in 1971. As gold was in such short supply, silver, which was more easily obtainable, became the basis of the coinage. A new coin, the denier, was minted, copying the silver currency used in the Caliphate of Spain. Although the denier was the only coin in actual circulation, for accounting purposes twelve deniers made a sous, and twenty sous made one livre. This system was adopted by the English king Offa, who was friendly with Charles the Great, and the silver penny became the popular coin in England for most of the Middle Ages. After the eleventh century the Italian gold florin was widely adopted as being more convenient in large transactions, but gold coinage did not become popular in England until the 'noble' was minted in the fifteenth century.

An improved currency helped the traders, but there remained all the dangers and inconveniences for the traveller in a static agrarian economy. To overcome these difficulties, merchants and traders of all origins formed themselves into a fraternity. Men of similar interests, or destinations, would band together for the journey. This afforded them mutual protection, and helped them to overcome the minor disasters, which were a common occurrence on the road. During the Dark Ages the sheer physical difficulties of travel were a deterent to trade, and these tended to deteriorate during the Middle Ages. The very roads themselves were a constant source of anxiety and annoyance. Since the overthrow of the Romans the knowledge of road building had disappeared, and there was no money, skill, or desire to build and repair roads. Slowly the mighty network of Roman military roads fell into decay. Bridges and viaducts collapsed, ditches silted up and flooded, the paved surfaces weathered and crumbled, and the untamed forest advanced, so that whole sections disappeared. Where new towns and villages had grown up away from Roman sites they could only be reached by unplanned earth tracks, which wound a haphazard course through the forests, and crossed rivers at the nearest ford.

In consequence it was impossible to reach anywhere quickly. Travel was, of necessity, a leisurely affair in an age when only the best mounted royal messenger could hope to cover thirty miles in a day. A heavily laden wagon, or a string of pack animals, were lucky if they could progress more than five miles in the daylight hours. Until the authorities came to appreciate the importance of commerce nothing was done to improve these conditions. Even then repair and maintenance work was crude and haphazard, except near the towns in whose interest it lay to speed communications.

The inevitable delays made it impossible for the trader to have a set timetable, or even itinerary, because long detours were often necessary: above all travel was seriously limited to certain parts of the year. The winter rains and frost turned the roads into a sea of mud, and the fords became raging torrents. This meant by the autumn the pedlars had to return to their homes, and spend the winter months in preparing for the next year. By the spring the roads had become usable, but were soon cut into deep ruts and potholes which were baked hard by the summer sun, and reduced traffic to the merest crawl. At the same time the traveller had to contend with the ankle-deep dust, which swirled up under the horses' hooves, and made travel so unpleasant. It was much more comfortable to travel by river and sea, but until the era of canal building this had its limitations, despite the shallow draught of ships, which enabled them to penetrate far up the tidal rivers. Wherever possible bulky goods such as stone or grain were carried by water, and short canals, or cuts, were often built to help in the building of castles and monasteries. These, however, did little to ease the hardships of the merchant.

In time the spontaneous companionship among the traders grew into a more organised bond. The pedlars began to form themselves into regular caravans in the same manner as desert travellers still do today. At first these groups were of mixed interests, but soon they began to specialise, forming fraternities, out of which the later guilds were to develop. These brotherhoods of the road were known as 'hanses', and were well armed, because as virtual outcasts they had to be prepared to protect themselves against all comers. The caravans had their own headquarters and routes, along which the stopping places were chosen carefully to coincide with the peak production periods of the regions. As trade expanded the hanses would have permanent bases, and the members would gradually acquire equal status with the communities of skilled craftsmen resident in the town. In this manner the travelling pedlar became accepted into society.

Just as the modern desert caravan moves from oasis to oasis, so their forerunners of the Dark Ages travelled between the towns. Apart from the obvious consideration that only in the urban centres was there sufficient demand, the authorities tried to enforce the laws restricting trade to these places. Practical necessities made it desirable for the merchant caravans to seek the shelter of the town walls before nightfall. Wayside inns and villages would not afford sufficient food, or shelter for a large party of travellers. Moreover they did not give very satisfactory protection against marauders, although even these were better than being benighted by the roadside. These two factors made it imperative for the merchants to plan their journeys by easy stages so that they could be sure of arriving at their destination in good time. In view of the uncertainty and lawlessness most town authorities imposed a curfew, under which the town gates were closed at dusk and only reopened in the morning, and all strangers had to be off the streets during the night. As the merchants had to arrive at a town at the correct time to take part in the scheduled trading, they were anxious not to be shut out of the town, or to have their preparations curtailed by the curfew.

To some extent these problems were less serious during this period because trading was still comparatively spontaneous, and was not hedged about by rigid regulations that were to develop later. There was little difference between fairs and markets, and the opportunities of the itinerant merchant were limited by local interests. No particular demarcation line had been drawn between retail and wholesale trade. Despite the growing circulation of silver coinage there had to be a considerable amount of barter. International distribution of essential consumer goods, such as iron, wine, grain and salt went on alongside the everyday trading in small surpluses from town to town. Specialisation had not yet become fully recognised, and everyone took part in the general commerce. This was somewhat chaotic and it became obvious that, if there was not to be a serious disruption to routine, more organisation was necessary. Gradually trade became more organised as the merchants and the authorities began to regulate the times and the methods of trading.

The needs of the merchants, craftsmen and the general public were not exactly similar, and commerce had to be adapted to meet their differing requirements. On a local level a weekly turn-over of trade was needed on a retail basis, whilst for the craftsmen and overseas merchant larger wholesale transactions were imperative. The feudal lords, both Church and State, recognised that trade was a source of much-needed taxation. Commerce, however, was outside the normal, tangible concept of taking rents for land, and a completely new structure had to be devised. In this manner a three-tier system of a commercial taxation was created, which was to set the pattern of trade during the Middle Ages. The greatest volume of trade was in the import and export of essential consumer goods, and to a large extent this passed through the sea ports.

Goods were taxed either as they came into the country, or prior to export. This formed an important part of the royal revenue, and had the great advantage of increasing with the growth of trade, in comparison with rents which remained comparatively static. The weekly turnover of trade in the market place provided a smaller, but steady source of taxation. Tolls had to be paid by people coming into a town to buy, or to sell, and a further toll had to be paid on the goods that were sold. During the Dark Ages the feudal owners of the towns tended to regard this money as their rightful due. As the towns became stronger the citizens were able to buy exemption from these tolls, or the right to keep them for the upkeep of the town. Nevertheless a percentage of these taxes went to the king, or to the local overlord. In any case the grant of such rights always provided the king with a large fee. The third tier of taxation was the fair, which, with the growth of commerce, attracted enormous crowds, and was a tremendous source of revenue.

It was from this line of thought that the market and the fair came into being. By the tenth century it had become evident that the town had to be treated differently from the normal feudal holding. The overlord of a town administered it through a bailiff, who was usually chosen from among the prominent townsmen. In time this bailiff and the other officials would form a ruling elite in the town. It was these people who would petition the overlord for the privileges of holding weekly markets, and in some cases the right to have a fair. This arrangement was beneficial to both parties, as it was easier to collect taxes, not only at designated places, but at set times. As fairs and markets attracted merchants, and so increased the volume of trade in a town, the overlord was only too pleased to see his revenue expanding. Until the twelfth century these rights and privileges were very haphazard, and very few records have survived. Even so the practice was well established before the end of the Dark Ages.

Commerce was becoming recognised as a respectable calling, and the Church had withdrawn much of its opposition. This was to have an important effect upon the status of the itinerant pedlars who had led a difficult life since the fall of the Roman Empire. The merchant was able to fill a respectable position within society, and during the medieval period the middle classes were to become ever more influential. The first effect of this change was that the pedlar, no longer a landless outcast, was able to settle down in the towns alongside the craftsmen industrialists, and became a master employer. As the towns became more concerned with their own interests and began to charge tolls for visiting traders, the itinerant found it advantageous to have a permanent place of residence. In this way they came to merge into the existing community, and were able to shape the growth of commerce.

The weekly market had become well established as a local event to serve the needs of a relatively small area in the immediate neighbourhood of the town. Country people were able to come into the town to buy the daily essentials which they could not make for themselves, and in turn sell, or barter their own farm produce. Well before the end of the Dark Ages both merchants, and towns-people were becoming dissatisfied with the scope of this type of trading. As an increasing number of tolls were levied against the visiting trader fewer itinerants visited the towns. The number of people, and the range of goods for sale, were too small to com-pensate the costs of travel and payment of taxes. The resident merchants themselves felt that they were isolated from the main avenues of trade, and town committees began to see the need to attract trade. Foreign merchants were unlikely to undergo the rigours of the road unless special inducements were made to make their journey profitable. It was from this need that the early chartered fairs were to evolve. The fair became extremely popular with all classes within the town and the surrounding countryside. To the ordinary people it offered a holiday, and the opportunity to buy luxuries at wholesale prices. The merchants, foreign and resident, benefitted from the tremendous turnover of trade which accompanied fairs; while the town authorities welcomed the large increase in revenue that resulted from the presence of a fairground.

These first chartered fairs were very primitive in comparison with the great fairs of the later Middle Ages. They were normally held within the walls of a town, because the times were too troubled and unsafe for them to take place in the open. This meant that fairs were on a very small scale. Sometimes they were held in market places and streets, but more frequently within a churchyard, or cathedral precinct. This might seem somewhat strange in view of the Church's opposition to trade, but at this stage paganism was still a serious threat to Christianity. The association of old cult festivals with saint days meant that gather-ings on these days had traditional links with heathenism. Con-sequently the Church preferred to keep Christianity constantly before the fairgoers, and so it was ideal to have the fair close to a church where the clergy could supervise the proceedings. At the same time the Church was anxious to foster peace, and to stress the sanctity of life. Thus the clergy attempted to preserve the peace and holiness traditional to such occasions. Out of this grew the conventions of the 'peace of the fair' and 'fair dealing'. This had a two-way effect, because although a high standard of behaviour and honesty was expected, the Church extended the privilege of sanctuary to the fairground. Even after the site of the fair moved away from the churchyard the notion of sanctuary remained so that all those attending the fair, except for notorious outlaws, were safe from arrest for crimes committed previously. It was this convention, which continued long after the fair had lost its connection with the Church, that led to the license and rowdiness of the later fairs.

The fairs of the early Middle Ages were not at first notable for the amount of trade that was carried out. The main concern of the townspeople and the local peasantry was to come into the church for services commemorating the saint's day, and then to enjoy the holiday with sports and games. Only gradually did the itinerant traders come in increasing numbers to set up their rough booths to sell trinkets to the holiday makers. Even by the end of the eleventh century the number of stalls did not seriously overcrowd the available space. It is true that the fairs might have extended into two or three days, but this was more a sign of the town authority's willingness to collect extra revenue, than a great expansion in the amount of trade. The pattern of the fair was established, however, and certain sites had become centres to which the merchants of distant parts were willing to visit every year. The fair was no longer just an event in the ecclesiastical calender, but a period when people from the whole locality could meet together. An occasion to exchange gossip, to meet 'foreigners' who could tell them news from distant parts, and a time when small luxuries could be bought at a reasonable price.

At the same time another type of fair was developing along entirely different lines. The growth of such fairs was the result of the expanding needs of local industry, and unlike their counterparts they were devoted entirely to commerce. When the merchant hanses visited town markets in search of local manufactured goods, they, naturally enough, soon learned where to find the best examples of certain goods. In the course of time particular areas became famous for their wool, cloth, glassware and other articles.

Such reputations spread quickly among the close-knit fraternity of the road, and the number of traders coming to these places steadily increased. For convenience there would be set times for this type of trading, and gradually the privileges of the fair were extended to them. In this manner the great speciality fairs developed, which, by the later Middle Ages, would last for over a fortnight, and catered exclusively for the wholesale trade. A good example of this type of fair was the Londoners' Fair at Bury St. Edmunds in Suffolk, which began well before the eleventh century. Bury St. Edmunds was the centre of a thriving local cloth-making industry which attracted the attention of the rich London merchants, who came every year to buy all the surplus cloth. From being a small street market this event became one of the most important East Anglian fairs of the early Middle Ages.

Thus by the tenth century the outcasts, pedlars and vagabonds who had kept the trickle of trade moving through the great stagnation of the Dark Ages had achieved a respectable position within the feudal society. These were the men who now formed an important part of the sturdy middle classes who were playing an ever-increasing part within the security of their town walls. This did not mean that the roads were becoming deserted. The wandering merchant might have become a settled freeman of a town, but travel was still the essence of trade. Indeed many merchants undertook long journeys themselves, especially to the important centres of commerce. Quite apart from this the merchant had become a master employer and continued to send out caravans under the command of his agents and servants. In any case with the return of comparative peace to Western Europe the roads became thronged with a motley band of vagrants, quacks, beggars, pilgrims and entertainers all on their way to, or from the ever-growing towns.

4   The Great Commercial Expansion

THE MEN of the hanse had achieved their position at just the right moment, because events in the Mediterranean were occurring which were to have a profound effect upon the development of trade and the fair. The cause of these changes was the great growth in the military strength of Christendom after the Viking invasions had been defeated. The war against the Moslems was now carried into the eastern Mediterranean, where the struggle for the control of the sea went in favour of the Italian city states. This conflict had long ceased to be purely religious, and had resolved itself into a contest for the control of the trade routes. The Republic of Venice by making an alliance with the Emperor at Constantinople was the first to re-establish contact with the Near East, but was soon challenged by the other Italian cities. Then at the end of the eleventh century Arabia was overrun by the fierce Seljuk Turks, who refused to allow Christian pilgrims to visit the holy places of Palestine. This led to the First Crusade, led by the princes of Western Europe, which reconquered Jerusalem, and established the Latin Kingdoms in Palestine. In return for transporting the crusaders the Italians gained exclusive trading rights with the new kingdoms and the Eastern Empire, although Venice kept her monopoly of trade with Constantinople. Suddenly, after a lapse of several centuries, the Mediterranean once more linked the West with the riches of the East.

To some extent northern Europe had already established a commercial contact with Constantinople through the Swedish Vikings, who like their Danish cousins were basically traders. They conquered the lands south-east of the Baltic and penetrated into the western lands of modern Russia, gaining control of the river crossings along the old Amber Way to the Black Sea. There they established strong twin capitals at Novgorod and Kiev, which gave them control of all the trade between the Baltic and Constantinople. Along these rivers came silk, spices, glassware, jewellery and many other luxuries previously so lacking in the West. In return grain, furs, wax, honey and amber were sent to the countries of the Near East. The Baltic soon became the centre of a European luxury trade, the merchandise of the Levant being distributed by the Viking pirates.

As the momentum of trade between the Baltic and the Black Sea increased the wealth of the new Swedish empire rose rapidly. Kiev and Novgorod, guarded by their massive kremlins, became two of the largest cities in Europe. Of the two Kiev developed the more quickly and, by the eleventh century, had eight markets and some forty churches. The building of Novgorod, new town, did not begin until the tenth century, but then it expanded very quickly, and within two hundred years it had outgrown Kiev, having its own 'gildehalle' and eight market places. The renewal of trade between Palestine and Italy depressed trade in Russia, especially as it came at the same time as a succession of civil wars in Scandinavia. To compensate for the decline in the Baltic trade the Russian cities began to specialise in craft industries such as metal working, jewellery, pottery, glassware, wood carving and textiles. In Kiev alone there were sixty craft guilds, and Russia became famed for its workmanship, which was a mixture of Byzantine and Scandinavian techniques. These Russian industries were to flourish for some two hundred years, then in the middle of the thirteenth century the country was devastated by the Mongol tribesmen from Central Asia, and Russia became an economic backwater — a country as remote to the West as distant China until it was rediscovered by English merchants in the sixteenth century.

Quite apart from the enterprise of the Swedish in reviving Baltic trade, the Vikings played an important part in the general reawakening of European trade. Their spirited independence and bustling commercialism did much to quicken the pace of town expansion. Equally Scandinavian seamanship and skill in ship-building did much to help in the reopening of the European seaways, and boosted many ports which had been steadily declining. Viking adventurers had explored the waters of the northern Atlantic, establishing settlements in Iceland and Green-land, and even along the east coast of North America five centuries before the voyages of Christopher Columbus. This versatility revitalised a stagnating Europe and encouraged the middle classes to explore fresh channels of trade. Moreover the Viking longship, once the terror of Europe, was to become the basis of medieval ships until the fifteenth century, making longer voyages more feasible. People began to travel with greater freedom, and international trade had become possible.

Despite the seemingly endless wars and devastation of the Dark Ages, which was prolonged by the Vikings, Europe emerged in a stronger position. The population, which had remained small since the fall of the birthrate in the old Roman Empire, began to increase steadily until it reached a peak in 1348, when the scourge of the Black Death reached the West. Within a year endemic bubonic plague had almost halved the population, and recurrent outbreaks of the disease kept it low until the epidemic died out in the seventeenth century. This initial growth in population, coupled with an improvement in farming techniques and industrial methods, enabled the production of larger surpluses. As the number of people in the villages increased there was considerable colonisation and clearance of forest and wasteland by the peasants. This development was extremely important to the growth of the Mediterranean trade, because the great cities of the Levant, such as Constantinople and Alexandria, needed a dependable supply of food and raw materials. Western Europe was at once a source of these supplies, and a market for manufactured goods, playing the same rôle as the colonies for an industrialised Europe in the nineteenth century. Venice, for instance, began as a group of villages specialising in fishing and salt evaporation, and it was the shipment of these essentials to Constantinople that was the beginning of the huge Venetian trading empire. Europe benefitted enormously from these exchanges, which brought in much needed bullion to boost the economy. At the same time the importation of eastern manufactured goods provided examples for the small European industries to copy and develop new techniques.

Events in the eastern Mediterranean helped the European economy in another entirely unexpected manner. When monetary values had collapsed in the West after the fall of the Roman government, the eastern, or Byzantine, part of the Empire had remained wealthy. The strength of the Byzantine gold standard had made the situation worse in Europe. Then in the eleventh century the invasion of Palestine by the Seljuk Turks had endangered Constantinople. The Emperor, Alexius, was forced to debase his coinage in order to meet the extra military costs. Until then the golden byzant had been the soundest coin in the Mediterranean, and this had made Constantinople the leading financial market in the West. The fall in value of the byzant helped to raise the exchange of the European currency, and made trading easier. This came just at the time of the renewal of trade links with the Levant, and helped the Italians to break into the eastern markets.

Contacts with the Levant were more important than the mere trading between the cities of the Near East and the backward countries of Europe. Palestine was the western terminus of the overland route from China and the Far East. Caravans brought silks, spices, ivory and precious stones of India and China across these desert wastes to sell to the empires of the Mediterranean. Control of this lucrative trade had fallen into the hands of the Arabs, who had established shipping routes to India through the Red Sea and then across the Indian Ocean. Until the thirteenth century the overland route was extremely perilous because of the uncertain temper of the loose confederation of the tribesmen living along the trackways. Then the nomadic Mongol tribes living near Samarkand, who had become united under the leadership of Ghengis Khan,* swiftly established an empire stretching from China to Russia. The Mongols were a tolerant race who allowed merchants to travel through their territories in safety. Although China continued to be the fabulous land of Cathay to the majority of Europeans, a few adventurous spirits found their way along the trackways to this mysterious country. Most of these travellers were missionaries who tried to introduce Christianity into the East. The most famous of these visitors to the East was Marco Polo, a Venetian merchant, who journeyed to China, and lived for many years at the court of Kubla Khan.† This route remained open for a hundred years, until the Ming Emperors regained control of China, and shut the frontiers to the hated Westerners.

Before the closure of the overland route into China the Arabs had devised another means of tapping Eastern trade. Their fleets virtually controlled the Indian Ocean and thus it was easy for them to establish a lucrative commerce with the great port of Calicut on the eastern coast of India. Calicut was the meeting place for merchants from all over the Far East, and the Arabs were able to buy all the silks, spices and other luxuries which were in such high demand in Europe. These goods were shipped back to Palestine and sold to the Italian merchants at an excessive profit for the Arab middlemen. Obviously these goods were extremely expensive in West, but they were otherwise unobtainable. Perhaps of even

---

*1162–1227.
†1216–1294 (grandson of Genghis Khan).

greater importance was the contact with the civilised world which did much to raise the standard of medieval life and culture.

At the same time a secondary trading area was developing in northern Europe. The origin of this commercial revival was the Russian trade from the Black Sea to the Baltic. With the disruption of Scandinavia by the tenth century civil wars, the control of this trade passed from the Vikings to the embryonic merchant communities of England and Flanders. At first Flanders with its long coastline and broad navigable rivers was most suited to benefit from this development. The Low Countries occupied a position that made them part of neither Germany, nor France, and the people had acquired an independence from the feudalism prevalent elsewhere on the Continent. For this reason the region was particularly suited to the growth of a vigorous town life free from the usual restrictions imposed by Church and State. Soon the Flemish towns became self-governing communes, with vigorous industries, the most important of which was clothmaking. The area under the influence of Flemish trade steadily expanded southwards through the Rhineland, until it linked up with the Mediterranean trading zone extending north across the Alps from Italy.

All over Europe the pulse of life was quickening as commerce began to flow along the roads, and into the cities which had been slowly dying since the collapse of the old Empire. Straggling, over-grown villages began to take advantage of their fine geographical position, to take their place beside their ancient neighbours as centres of the new commercialism. Trade was no longer an outcast, and the merchant could take his place in society to rub shoulders with bishop and baron. A great class struggle was beginning that was to last throughout the Middle Ages, as trade and the merchant gradually supplanted feudalism and the nobleman.

Town and Guild

THE GROWTH of the fair followed swiftly upon the revitalisation of the town. One important sign of the new life in the urban area was the appearance of the guilds. All over Europe the standard of living was rising, and led to a higher demand for consumer goods and luxuries. With the increase in trade there was a slow but steady growth in the amount of money in circulation. This, in turn, caused a slow decline in feudalism, and a change from subsistence farming to capitalism. Such changes coincided with the rise in population, and resulting in a greater output, enabled more people to devote their time to other pursuits than farming. All over Europe there appeared fortified towns, castles, monasteries and other religious communities, all of which depended to a greater, or lesser, degree upon supplies from outside. It was this situation that helped the rapid growth of the craft guilds, the members of which organised commerce, and helped to foster retail and whole-sale dealing.

Guilds had been known in the towns for several centuries, but the early associations were mainly of a religious, or social nature. Although it is true that that the later guilds had important social and religious aspects in their organisation, their main function was the control of trade. The first guilds of this type to appear were general amalgamations of all trade groups within a town. This came as a natural result of the fraternisation among the pedlars and traders of the hanses. When the pedlars had become recognised as respectable merchants within town society they were anxious to win the right to trade freely from the owner of the town. Such grants were obtained through the payment of a sizeable fee to the owner, and took the form of a charter of free-burgage to the free-men of the town. An important clause in such agreements was one giving permission for the burgesses to have a 'hanshus', a hall where the caravaners could meet together. It was to such men that fell the task of organising the expanding economy of the towns, and in time the hanshus was to become the Town Hall.

These early organisations of the eleventh century were known as the Gild Merchants, and represented all branches of industry and trade. Thus it fell to the members to do all in their power to foster all aspects of commerce. Apart from being concerned with the smooth running of trade within the town, the Wardens and Aldermen were responsible for obtaining more grants and privileges for their town. It was these men who obtained the initial grants allowing the holding of markets and fairs, or, at least, had earlier rights confirmed by written charters. The days of the Gild Merchant were limited, and within a century their place was taken by other organisations. As more trades and skills blossomed under the protective walls of town and castle, the early unity disappeared. Trade was now accepted, and the merchants no longer needed mutual protection. Jealousies and rivalry developed as each trade strove to gain a share of the available market. One Gild Merchant could no longer serve the interests of the many, and gradually separate craft guilds were born out of the parent body. Although its original purpose had gone the Gild Merchant survived as governing committee in a town, composed of representatives from the main craft guilds. Eventually this body became strong enough in many towns to elect its own mayor and corporation, which was the mark of the final emancipation of the town from the feudal system.

The new, small but powerful craft guilds now controlled commerce within the towns. Their objectives differed widely from the purpose of the early trade organisations. Towns no longer needed to attract merchants and trade, their main problem was to protect the residents from undue competition from outside. For this reason almost every craft and trade had its own guild, which was expected to maintain the interests of its members. Membership was only open to master craftsmen and freemen of the town, and one of the main objectives of a guild was to maintain a maximum wage. As the Middle Ages progressed the guilds became extremely exclusive, and only the owners of considerable urban property, or the sons of existing guildsmen could gain admittance. At the same time, however, all members were expected to maintain a very high standard of workmanship and quality of material. 'Searchers' were appointed by the guild officials to inspect the premises, and goods of all members to ensure compliance with these rules. To protect guildsmen from 'foreigners' and 'interlopers', who undercut on retail trade, it was made very difficult for outsiders to trade within a town. In time these considerations led to such a multitude of regulations that trade was strangled in the older towns, and the guilds themselves collapsed.

Although the guilds had a detrimental effect upon the freedom of urban trade they did much to facilitate the fair. To a large extent this was accidental. By making it very difficult for outside merchants to trade, or to settle, within a town, the guilds created a self-perpetuating community of freemen. At the same time by charging high tolls on goods coming into the town, and large stallage fees for those who wished to sell in the market, residents always had a great advantage over visitors. These conditions prevailed all over Europe so that merchants had to be very wealthy, or have very influential connections, to be able to break the local monopolies of the guilds. It was this atmosphere of restriction that made the fair such a welcome break in the normal conditions. There was an urgent need for free movement to encourage the growth of international trade, and for this reason the fair became the focal point of medieval commerce. The period of the fair was a time when visiting merchants were welcomed to a town, even by the guilds, and thus a continuous flow of trade was maintained in Europe.

During the eleventh century, however, the fair had yet to establish itself. This was the period when the market, the direct ancestor of the fair, was becoming important. One of the earliest of the privileges obtained by the members of the Gild Merchant was the right to hold weekly markets. At first it was usual for there to be one market place sited near the hanshus where it could be supervised by the officers of the Gild Merchant. As trade expanded this arrangement became unsatisfactory as the original market place became too small, and there was a need for specialised markets. In due course it became normal for the larger towns to hold several markets during the week at special designated points. The original right to hold a market placed the casual trading of the Dark Ages on an official basis, so that the profits could be shared between the town government and the owner of the town. The establishment of the specialist markets was a sign of the growing influence of the craft guilds, which gradually gained control over the markets. Certain days and places were set aside for the sale of different commodities, each town having its own particular arrangements. Such organisation was a practical necessity, as it was difficult to carry merchandise through the narrow and busy streets. For this reason the fishmarket, and wholesale market for heavy goods, would be held near the riverside quays and warehouses. Otherwise only the market place situated near the Guild Hall would be a large open space with semi-permanent booths, the remainder were street markets where the specialist craftsmen normally congregated. The main market place was strictly supervised by the officials of the town government, while the street markets were more under the control of guild officers.

It was essential for the guilds in their efforts to protect the public and their own members to keep a strict check upon the markets. To a large extent their task was not too difficult in an age of rapid commercial expansion and a limited skilled labour force. Entry into a craft could be rigorously controlled through apprenticeship, as it was possible to restrict the number of apprentices which master craftsmen were allowed to train. In most cases, once an apprentice had qualified he had to work as a journeyman for a number of years to earn enough money to set up as a master craftsman. As such journeymen were only allowed to work under special licenses, their number could be controlled by the guild officials. It was less easy for the guild officers to maintain such a rigid control over the market. Outside merchants were not welcomed at the market, but the town was a market centre for the locality so it was not possible to exclude all strangers. For this reason there developed a body of commercial law, which, although basically uniform, differed in each locality in order to meet the individual needs of each town.

These laws were compiled gradually during the course of the Middle Ages. In the first place a set of laws were drawn up by the Gild Merchants, and these formed the foundation of a town's commercial law. Then with the development of the craft guilds, each of these drew up a set of laws covering the special needs of their craft. These were then added to the original town laws to comprise a comprehensive merchant code. The primary consideration of the laws was the protection of the resident merchants, and to ensure a high degree of honesty. Thus the resident ratepayer, a freeman who was in 'scot and lot', having paid his scot, or rates, had preference over any outsider when making bargains, or lots. Any stranger who struck a bargain for a consignment of merchandise had to allow a resident to share in the lot at the same price. The guilds benefitted in a similar manner, because they were allowed to share in any lots of raw materials used in their craft. The person who originally struck the bargain was allowed to keep at least a quarter of the whole consignment, but at the same time he was responsible for paying the entire cost to the owner. Those sharing in a bargain had to pay their quota within twenty-four hours, or had to return the goods to the original purchaser. This meant that travelling merchants had to be well versed in the laws of the towns which they visited, or they would soon find themselves in trouble with the courts.

Such laws made it imperative that there was strict supervision, and that hours of marketing had to be carefully observed. No trading was allowed before the officials had rung the market bell, and all dealing ceased directly the bell marked the hour of closure. Certain people were entitled to inspect and buy goods before the opening of the market. This right of pre-emption was vested in the king and the owner of the town, and their representatives were allowed to reserve any lots in which they were interested. Other people could buy similar rights of pre-emption. Monasteries and other religious houses frequently took advantage of this privilege, because of the need to buy in bulk to provide for large households. Whilst these preliminaries were taking place the market officials had to keep a sharp watch to ensure that there was no 'forestalling', selling to unauthorised people before market hours, or 'regratting', buying at wholesale prices with the intention of later retail sale.

In these boisterous times it was found necessary not only to segregate the main crafts into separate street markets, but group each craft and trade into its own quarter in the main market place. These precautions did much to lessen the likelihood of brawls between rival guilds. Any strangers who came to the market to sell goods had to set up their stall in the area assigned to their particular craft, where they were kept under strict supervision. Any stranger wishing to sell his goods outside the official market had to have a sponsor, who was a resident freeman of unblemished reputation. The stranger was then allowed to sell his merchandise on the premises of his 'host', who was entirely responsible for the stranger's debts, conduct and honesty. To compensate for this the sponsor could claim a half share of any lots sold in his house.

Throughout the Middle Ages the essence of market trading was that all sales had to be made before witnesses to ensure that there was no malpractice. Great emphasis was placed upon the need for complete probity in all dealing, and there were always a large number of officials present at any market to enforce the regulations. In all towns the State continued to hold certain rights of justice and taxation. This usually meant that custom dues, tunnage and poundage, and poll taxes were paid to the local royal officials, property taxes and local dues were kept by the town, who paid a percentage to the owner of the town. There was a similar division of the fines imposed in the town courts. Criminal cases were tried by royal officers with the fines going to the Crown, while civil cases were under the jurisdiction of the town courts. This meant that as there was no freedom of arrest at markets, both civic and royal officials had to be present. In any case the State had wide powers of supervising many aspects of trade carried on within towns. All manufactured goods were liable to inspection by royal officers for the purpose of taxation and, especially in the case of wool and cloth, had to carry royal seals before sale. Each town had to have its Assize of Bread and Ale, and Weights and Measures, and any merchant was liable to be brought before the court to test the weight and quality of his goods. In many cases royal officers were selected from among the leading residents of a town, and were members of the town council, or one of the guilds.

Before trading began the officials had to make sure that everything was ready. Each town had its own routine so that these preliminaries were not so complicated as might appear. All goods had to be inspected before dealing began, to ensure that they complied with the standards, and that there was no stolen property. Officials with standard weights and measures stationed themselves at convenient points in case of disputes between buyers and sellers. With them were Market Supervisors who tried to settle any disputes; if this was impossible the disputants were taken to the nearest court. The supervisors were responsible for maintaining order, deploying the ward constables to arrest trouble-makers, and to break up any brawls. Another of their duties was to make sure that business ran smoothly by providing enough porters with sledges and baskets to maintain a rapid flow of goods from the stalls. The sledges and baskets were necessary because in many towns wheeled carts were banned as their iron rims broke up the streets. Trading ended with the ringing of the market bell, when the 'scavengers' and 'rakers' set about clearing up the piles of rubbish left in the streets.

On market days the country people would begin to make their way towards the town well before dawn. Most of them came on foot carrying loads of farm produce, or driving a few cattle, sheep and pigs. The wealthier yeoman farmers might come with a cart, or on horseback. With them would come the pedlars and traders who had been unable to reach the town before the evening curfew. On arrival at the town gates they would be stopped by chains stretched across the roadway, which would only be lifted by the watchmen after the payment of toll. The amount would depend upon the mode of travel and the goods being carried. This might cause some delay because some people might claim to be exempt from toll and this had to be checked. The money collected in this way normally went into the town's 'murage', or 'pavage' funds, which were used to keep the walls and streets in repair. 'Foreigners' coming into the town to sell goods were directed to the areas occupied by their respective crafts, or, in some towns, to the quarter set aside for outside merchants. A close watch was kept on their activities, especially the 'snarlers' and 'hawkers', wandering pedlars, because it was felt that they were probably dealing in stolen goods.

The times of opening for the market would vary with the season, and during the summer months trading would begin very early. This was due partly to the Norman laws of curfew preventing all unauthorised people from being on the streets during the hours of darkness, but mainly because the lack of effective artificial lighting made it impossible to start business before daylight. For most of the Middle Ages a great part of the market trading was carried out through barter. The reason for this was the chronic shortage of ready cash especially among the peasantry who were the main buyers at the market. Only the wealthier yeoman farmers made their transactions in cash. The majority of the country people would barter their farm produce in return for the necessities, such as salt, leather and cloth, needed for their daily existence. The few pence which they could save were hoarded to buy large items such as a new cow, an iron cooking pot, or some small luxury at the annual fair.

Market days were scenes of bustling confusion and the officials were kept very busy settling disputes, or arresting brawlers and pickpockets. Any serious breaches of the peace were dealt with by the ordinary courts, and offenders were lodged in the town goal to await their hearing. At the same time the magistrates held special courts to deal with minor cases in a summary fashion to avoid delays. The most common offence was selling short measure, and, as this offence was prevalent throughout Europe, only serious cases were ever brought to court. Anyone discovered giving short measure, or selling inferior goods was taken before the Inspectors of Weights and Measures, and then taken by the constables to be placed in the stocks, or pillory. They were then left until nightfall and passers-by were free to pelt them with whatever refuse came to hand. Another frequent cause of dispute was the ownership of goods. In disputes over stolen goods the owner had to bring an action in court against the person in whose possession the goods were found. If the accused could bring reliable witnesses to testify that he bought the articles in good faith, he was allowed to keep them, or to sell them back to the owner at the same price as he had paid for them. Breach of contract was another matter which often led to court actions. In this case the dispute was usually decided by which of the contestants could produce the greater number of witnesses to support his assertions. The main difficulty here was to decide what constituted a contract. Well before the end of the Middle Ages it had become generally accepted that a handshake was legal proof that a contract had been made. Minor cases of this nature with a certain amount of drunkenness and malicious wounding were the main work of the courts and it was unusual for more serious offences to occur.

It has already been seen that not all trading was carried out in the official market places. Resident merchants were entitled to use their houses, or business premises, for marketing, providing that they were prepared to take full responsibility for any misdemeanours that might occur. In a similar manner there developed a number of highly specialised markets which had nothing to do with the retail trading which was open to the general public. These types of transaction had their own regulations, and were supervised by officials appointed by the Town Council and the guilds. They were more closely linked with the affairs of the craft guilds than with the ordinary markets because they dealt with trade goods, such as leather, wine, cloth and wool, and were attended almost exclusively by members of the craft. Such 'marts' were frequently held in the houses of merchants, or in rooms specially set aside in the Town Hall and the craft livery hall. The goods for sale were in bulk and were at wholesale prices, and this was a method of keeping industry flowing throughout the year. Craftsmen were able to maintain their stocks of raw materials, and semi-finished goods, without having to rely solely on the annual fair. This type of market was an essential link with the wholesale dealing at the fairs.

6   The Early Chartered Fairs

THE TOWN had become a close-knit society of such an exclusive nature that the fair was placed in a somewhat anomalous position. Everyone recognised the need for annual fairs, but burgesses and guildsmen were jealous of their local rights, and were very antagonistic towards visiting merchants. The high tolls levied by the town authorities and the petty regulations of the guilds were difficult to escape, and so visitors tended to become discouraged. Bad feeling was created and the existing fairs became notorious for the brawls and bloodshed between resident and visiting traders. At this point the whole organisation of the fair might have collapsed if the great number of people attending them had not represented a large, potential source of income. In the eleventh century the towns were only just beginning to acquire the freedom and power which they were to wield later in the Middle Ages. The Crown and the feudal nobles still exercised considerable authority, and it was due to their influence that many of the great chartered fairs came into being.

The main consideration with the creation of the medieval fair was to ensure that they were attractive to the resident merchant community, and that people from outside were able to attend without interference. This became an increasingly important factor as the power of guilds imposed an ever stronger stranglehold over the commercial freedom of the towns, and nepotism created closely knit ruling oligarchies. To overcome restrictions encountered by visiting merchants, especially those from overseas, there had to be sufficient inducement to attract them to the fairground. Fortunately many merchants in the guilds realised that over-restriction was stultifying trade within the towns, and were prepared to welcome the development of the fairs. Even as early as the twelfth century many of the older towns were already in decline, and were being deserted by the more independent craftsmen, who resented the control by a reactionary minority. The decline of such towns coincided with the growing importance of the fairs. With the growth in European international trade it became clear that the towns, although a vital link, were not the ideal location for the transaction of the wider Continental commerce. Thus some of the earliest of the chartered fairs were to be seen in the areas where the Flemish and Italian trading zones overlapped. A two-tier system was evolved in which fairs, although attached to towns, were free from the petty restrictions that were beginning to cripple urban commerce.

Kings and nobles were equally eager to share in the profits to be made from the greater freedom of movement which became possible after the ending of the Dark Ages. This mobility was by no means restricted to merchants. With the recapture of Jerusalem pilgrimages had become very fashionable, not only to the Holy Places, but equally to more locally famous shrines of national saints. To those with business acumen it was obvious that a coalescence of trade and pilgrimages would be extremely lucrative. The people best situated to take advantage of this were the great ecclesiastical princes who wielded wide ecclesiastical and secular authority. Not only were such men ideally placed to know which shrines were likely to attract the most pilgrims, but unlike the State the Church often maintained a close control over its towns well into the Middle Ages. This is well reflected in the development of the early chartered fairs on the Continent, where the influence of the Church was even stronger than in England.

The main avenues of commerce in the eleventh century were Palestine to Italy and from thence to the Netherlands: the northern and southern trading areas meeting and merging in the Rhineland. With the colonisation of eastern Germany following the crusades of the Teutonic Knights, the Baltic was to revive as a key commercial region. To the west of the Rhine Spain and particularly France had emerged as prime wine producing countries, and wine was rapidly becoming one of the staple items of medieval trade. Finally to the north was England, for so long isolated from the Continent, but with the Norman conquest rapidly becoming important as a producer of high quality wool. Much of this commerce was carried through fleets of small coasting vessels which, despite the unseaworthiness of medieval ships, and the lack of navigational aids, could sail from the North Sea to the Mediterranean by following coastal landmarks. This method of distribution had its limitations, despite the shallow draughts of the ships which enabled them to penetrate well inland along the tidal rivers. Even transhipment to barges did not allow merchandise to be taken to those parts distant from navigable waters. This meant that the cart and the packhorse still played an important rôle. In any case travel by water was an extremely slow and laborious process. Merchants had to rely upon both road and river, and consequently those areas well served by both were ideal sites for fairs.

The Rhine being the largest river in Western Europe, with a hinterland well served by Roman roads, it is not surprising that the first important fairs sprang up in this area. The Rhineland which linked Italy and the Netherlands was a strip of neutral territory separating the Empire from France. By the twelfth century the Jews who had pioneered this trade route had largely been replaced by the Lombards. The wealth of the Levant trade passed through the hands of Venice and the other city-states to the towns of the Lombardy plain, from whence it was carried through the St Gothard and Mount Cenis passes into southern France. Apart from the trade with the Levant the Italians benefitted by learning some of the secrets of the Near Eastern industries, particularly clothmaking. Many Italian towns began to specialise in the production of silk and high quality woollen fabrics. The main difficulty faced by the Italians was to procure wool of suitable staple to maintain their standards. For this reason the Florentines became very interested in the parallel, but entirely unconnected, cloth industries in the Netherlands. The northern expansion from Italy was accelerated, and soon Italian merchants were mingling with the northern merchants in the Low Countries.

It was in the Low Countries that the first truly international fairs were to take place. These fairs were closely connected with the Flemish cloth industry and were held in the well established cloth towns, such as Ypres, Lille and Bruges. Merchants from all over Europe attended these events, being attracted mainly by the reputation of the Flemish weavers. The Italians, however, were not interested in the cloth, but in the source of the Flemings' wool supplies. They soon discovered that the Netherlands was poor sheep country. and produced little wool, their high quality wool being imported from England. It did not take the Italians long to cross the Channel and to penetrate the English wool markets. Once established the Italians maintained a privileged position in England until the fourteenth century, mainly due to their ability to make large loans to the Crown. Meanwhile the Flemish fairs had begun to decline. The reason for this was partially their close association with the old industrial towns with their rigid guild regimes, which tended to deter the visiting merchants. Many traders felt the need for fair sites which were not closely connected with any large town, and were free from restrictions. The Holy Roman Emperor,

Frederick II, was quick to realise the potential value of the streams of merchants passing through the Rhineland, which at this time had passed into his control. In 1231 he ordered the minting of the 'augustale' the first current gold coin in Western Europe, since the King Pepin had transferred from a gold to a silver standard. At the same time he ordered that sites should be made available in the Rhineland where annual fairs could be held.

By the thirteenth century the Champagne country was firmly established as the centre of the first truly international fairs of the Middle Ages. Here, at Troyes, Bar, Provins, Lagny and Bar-sur-Aube, developed a cycle of fairs which collectively lasted for most of the year. The Champagne area was for a century to be the centre of European commerce, a mecca to the merchants of the Western world. It is significant that this region was under the control of the Empire which was less restrictive than many of the feudal governments, and that the influence of the Church was very strong. None of the towns associated with the fairgrounds were under the influence of strong urban communes, so that there were fewer restrictions than in the older centres. In this atmosphere of commercial freedom these fairs were to flourish, until they were blighted by the Hundred Years War between England and France. It was here that many of the characteristics of the later fairs were to be created, and the pattern of international commercial law formulated. Indeed so famous were some of these fairs that their influence can be felt even today. The town of Troyes became a renowned centre for the goldsmiths and jewellers, and their measurements for precious metals became universally accepted as 'troy weight'.

The growth of this chain of fairs in the Rhineland had an important effect upon the development of the chartered fair in England. The importance of English wool as a major export had been realised, and England was firmly linked with the major thoroughfare of European trade. The success of the Champagne fairs emphasised the economic advantages of this type of commercial gathering. Once the Church had overcome its original aversion to trade, it was quick to realise the financial potential of the fair. At this time the co-operation between Church and State was still relatively close, and many of the first chartered fairs were granted to churchmen. This reflects the wealth and the power of the Church at this time, which was often in sharp contrast with the poverty of the Crown. This meant that

54

Churchmen, both regular and secular, could afford to buy costly charters, and the outlay necessary to set out a fairground. It was at this time that many of the semi-official, almost casual, meetings of the Dark Ages received royal sanctions.

The connection with the Church maintained the religious associations of the fair, and had practical advantages. The chartered fair was frequently held close to one of the great cathedrals, or monasteries. Such places usually housed the shrines which became popular attractions for the many pilgrims of the Middle Ages, and so provided the nucleus of the crowds to fill the fairground. At the same time the great religious houses supported a large number of inmates, whose needs could be fulfilled more cheaply by purchasing supplies at wholesale fair prices. It was quite common for religious houses to recoup royal debts by accepting the right to hold a fair. In a like manner the position was sometimes reversed; a royal chartered fair being given specifically to support a leper house, or hospital. Thus it was, quite apart from the earlier pagan supersitions, that the fair developed under the protection of the Church, and became surrounded with a certain aura of sanctity, which separated it from ordinary commercial dealings. For a time many of the chartered fairs continued to occupy the sites within the church-yard and cathedral precinct adopted during the Dark Ages. Then in the twelfth century the Vatican issued instructions forbidding this practice on the grounds that the immorality and rowdiness of the fair was detrimental to the clergy. Furthermore it was felt that such scenes taking place within the actual precincts of a church were a serious distraction from the solemnity of holy days.

Even without this ruling other considerations made it desirable that the fairground should be moved to a site outside the towns, or at least to a more commodious position. The rapid increase in trade made it impracticable for large numbers of people to have to make their way through narrow twisting streets to an equally tiny space in the centre of the town. It was equally necessary in many cases for the fairground to be removed from the influence of the guilds, which were becoming too exclusionist. Moves of this type did not sever the link with the Church, which continued until the sixteenth century. This influence became embodied in the universally accepted 'peace of the fair'. A fair was recognised as being set aside from normal, everyday affairs, and was freed from normal jurisdiction. Not only was the commercial law at the fair adapted to meet special requirements, but the fairground was placed outside the writ of royal officials enforcing criminal and civil law. As previously stated, all people attending a fair were immune from arrest for crimes previously committed, the only exception being outlaws and traitors. Such immunity did not apply to crimes committed during the course of the fair, which were dealt with by the fair officials.

To a certain extent the reason for this relaxation of the law was to protect visiting merchants who could have fallen foul of guild and borough law, and might have deterred them from coming to the fair. In the main, however, it was due to the Church's insistence that the clergy and ecclesiastical property should be immune from State courts that led to the exemption of the fairground. As the fairground was under the protection of the Church this immunity was applied to fairs held in the churchyard. The removal of the fair to another site did not end this privilege, indeed the extent of immunity was gradually increased. To protect those coming to the fair all approach roads had the same rights as the actual fairground, and in time the whole area within a radius of three miles was free from the royal writ for the duration of the fair. This relaxation was a cause of a great deal of laxity, and fairs became extremely unruly, with a notorious reputation for drunkenness and debauchery. At the same time the fairground was a major attraction for all the pickpockets and minor criminals in that part of the country, who could reckon on rich hauls from the visitors without much danger to themselves. As, however, the object of the fair was to get as many people as possible to spend the maximum amount of money, the authorities turned a benign eye to the excesses.

The fair had become recognised as an event set outside the course of normal life: a time of peace and goodwill in the midst of an otherwise violent and bloody age. Indeed it was not unknown for temporary truces to be arranged in time of war so that a fair could be held unmolested. The internationally recognised fair had become an essential link in the pattern of Continental trade. Even into the hard business world of commerce the special aura of tradition and religion influenced the working of the fair. The conduct of business at a fair was considered to have special significance beyond the ordinary honesty expected at the market. 'fair dealing' denoted that deals and contracts made at a fair had greater meaning, and were more binding than those made elsewhere.

) 'Cock throwing'—A traditional country sport on Shrove Tuesday. *Old England*

i) The dance of 'Bessie and the Clown'. A Plough Monday frolic that still survives in parts of the north of England. *Old England*

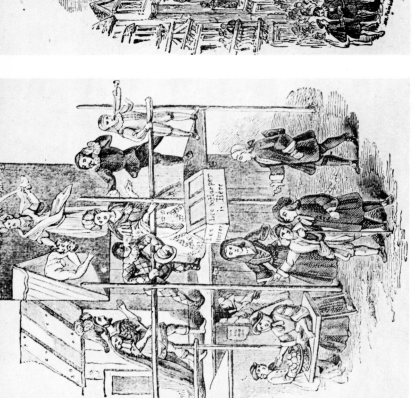

(iii) Lee and Harper's Booth at Bartholomew Fair, an example of the contrived spectacles of the eighteenth century.

Old England

(iv) May-pole dancing, one of the well known traditional dances.

Old England

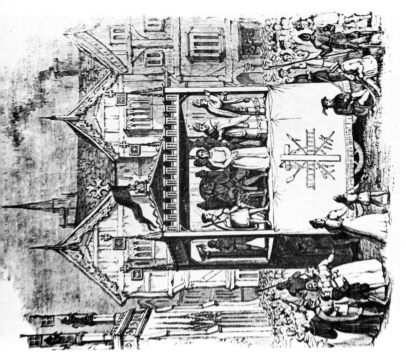

(vi) Mystery plays enacted by the craft guilds were great attractions.
This performance was at Coventry.

Old England

(v) Playing at Bucklers. Maids dancing for Garlands. *Old England*

(vii)   Pot Fair, Cambridge—A cruel caricature of the eighteenth century. Note the two headed 'droll' on the right.

Cambridge City Librar

(viii)   Tournaments were one of the great spectacles of the Middle Ages.   Old Engla

) Dancing Dolls, as pictured by Hogarth at Southwark Fair, and the Posture-Master. Two of the new attractions of the late eighteenth century fair. *Old England*

Milkmaids' Dance, with a pile of Plate, on May Day. *Old England*

(xi)   The Mummers were to be found at every medieval fair.   *Old Engla*

(xii)   Playing Bears, another feature of the fair.   *Old Engla*

(xiii)   A Stourbridge Fair booth of the eighteenth century. *Cambridge City Libraries*

v)   Garlic Row, once one of the great thoroughfares of Stourbridge, and Mercers Row still remembered despite modern expansion.   *D. J. Floyd*

(xv)   Morris dancing at Finchingfield, Essex—part of the ''Thaxted Ring'' that attracts Morrismen from all over England.   *D. J. Floy*

(xvi)   A fair ground today.   *D. J. Floy*

7   The Establishment of English Fairs

IMMEDIATELY after the Norman conquest of 1066 foreign merchants began to come to England in greater numbers than at any time since the departure of the Romans. Foremost of these newcomers were the Jews, and the Flemings, who emigrated in large numbers to settle in East Anglia, where they revitalised the native cloth industry. At first it was the arrival of the Jews that was to give the original impetus to the English fair. Jewish merchants following on the heels of the Norman invaders soon established themselves in a strong position in England by becoming bankers to the Anglo-Norman kings. Royal favour gave them freedom of movement and exemption from many taxes and tolls. They travelled widely and it was their presence at what had previously been localised fairs, that first gave national importance to several fairgrounds. The Jews were not popular, and with the growth of European banking houses they were soon superseded by the Italian Lombards. This was quickly followed by the withdrawal of royal favour, and they were expelled from the country.

In the long term it was the Flemings who proved to be the greatest boost to the development of the fair in England. The Flemings had come to England from the great cloth towns of the Low Countries in search of freer conditions in which to work. They had brought with them the expertise of Flanders, and their arrival brought the realisation of the value of English wool. For a short time several English towns became famous for their clothmaking, but this was only transitory. The Crown was more interested in the vast revenue to be made from the export of wool, and it was another two centuries before clothmaking became the great industry of England. Of greater immediate importance was the establishment of firm trading contacts with the Low Countries just at the time when the Lombards were beginning to dominate the Flemish wool and cloth fairs. Finding little good quality wool in Flanders the Italians soon crossed to England, and began to visit the wool sales in East Anglia and the West Country. Italian fleets especially from Genoa, began to call regularly at London, and several of the great Italian banking families opened offices in England.

The Italian merchants were wealthy so that they, and their agents, were able to tour the country buying up a large proportion of the best English wool for several years in advance. For this reason they dealt mainly with the monastic farm bailiffs who ran huge flocks in the north and the west of England. At the same time the Italians acted as bankers to the Plantagenet Kings, and took over the privileges and exemptions formerly held by the Jews. This had an enormous effect upon the English fair. The high production of wool created a very favourable balance of trade, which enabled England to import large quantities of foreign goods. At the same time it caused a steady increase in the standard of living, which in turn created a higher demand and purchasing power in England. The Italians with their control of the Levant trade, and their wide freedom of travel within England were well placed to supply these needs. As the English towns were controlled by the guilds who resented foreign merchants, the fair became the obvious centre of exchange.

While these changes were taking place in England the Flemish fairs had declined, and those in the Champagne were fast reaching their zenith. Thus until the fourteenth century the English fairs were overshadowed by their Continental counterparts, but thereafter they surpassed anything that had been seen in Europe. Some of the most famous of the early fairs were closely linked with towns, and their origin derived from Anglo-Saxon times. It is equally easy to find examples which owe their origin to the movement of industry and craftsmen away from the towns in the thirteenth century. In some cases a great fair grew out of a minor local gathering for the sale of animals. Indeed it is difficult to find one single cause for the growth of a particular fair, as it was a combination of several factors. Perhaps the easiest way in which to follow the growth of the English fair is to trace the origins of some of the most famous examples.

St Giles Fair, Winchester, which was to become the second largest of the great medieval fairs, is an excellent example of the complexity of derivation. From Prehistoric times Long Barrow had been a meeting place for religious festivals, and a famous landmark. With the growth of trade during the Bronze Age the barrow made a convenient meeting place at the junction of the Tin Way from Cornwall and the Gold Way from Wales on the route leading to the South Downs. The importance of the site continued under the Romans when the town of Venta grew up to benefit from the trade along these routes. The West Saxons reoccupied the site, and eventually made it the capital of their kingdom. Then when England became united under Athelstan in the tenth century, Winchester became the capital of England: a position it was to hold until Henry II eventually fixed the capital at Westminster in the twelfth century. Prior to this the second Norman king, William II, granted the Bishop of Winchester the right to hold an annual fair on the site below the Long Barrow. The reason for the grant was to enable the bishop to complete the building of Winchester cathedral. In the first place this was a confirmation of a Saxon fair, and lasted for three days following 31st August. Henry II extended the duration of the fair to sixteen days. Winchester's ancient traditions, coupled with its proximity to the Channel ports, placed it in an ideal position to share in England's re-entry into Continental trade.

Another of the fairs with a long history was St Cuthbert's at Durham. As its name suggests it was pre-Norman in its origin, and is perhaps one of the really large fairs which can trace its history directly back to these early times. It is an excellent example of a pagan festival becoming closely associated with a Christian feast day. During the early Dark Ages Durham and the Forests of Elmet were fiercely contested by the invading Angles, and the British Christians of Strathclyde. Yet it was missionaries from Strathclyde who finally converted the Northumbrians to Christianity. There followed a period of bitter fighting between the Northumbrians and the heathen Mercians, which eventually isolated the northern part of the kingdom. Thus Durham became the centre for the festival of St Cuthbert, one of the best known of the northern saints. Throughout the Middle Ages Durham formed part of the English defences along the Scottish marches; an area of constant feuds and border forays. Gradually the feast day of St Cuthbert, and the fair which had grown up with it became annual truce, where the retainers of rival nobles and princes could mingle peacefully for a short time. Surrounded by great areas of moor and upland grazing, the fair became famed for its livestock, hides and wool, which attracted both the wool dealers, and the stockrearers of the home counties.

Another well known fair at Chester had similarities to both Winchester and Durham. During the Roman conquest of Britain

Chester had become one of the great legendary fortresses for the conquest of Wales, and later for policing the western highlands. Its strategic importance caused the Saxons to refortify the town as a border defence in their long wars with the Welsh. Until Edward I conquered Wales in the fourteenth century it was a scene of constant raids and border forays by the Welsh. Gradually, however, the Welsh came to realise that they could benefit from the annual Chester fair, and began to mingle peacefully with the other visitors. They brought their upland sheep, and fleeces to sell, and in return bought some of the Continental luxury goods coming into England. This and the other border fairs were extremely important to the economy because the West Country produced the best quality wool in England. In consequence the agents of the manufacturers of high class cloth came to the fairs from all over England and the Continent.

The growing economic importance of the south of England, and in particular East Anglia and the home counties, became more obvious during the twelfth century. In this area was concentrated the bulk of the country's population and industry, while the north with its poor soil could only support a sparse population, and little industry. This distinction can be seen in the development of the fair, in that the two great international fairs, which were to dominate England and the Continent for the remainder of the Middle Ages, were situated in this area. These fairs were created out of the declining commercial influence of the town, and were a sign of desire by international merchants to seek freer trading of the type developed in the Champagne.

In 1100, only six years after the Winchester charter, Henry I, the younger brother of William II, granted the township of Slepe in Huntingdonshire the right to hold an annual fair. The reason behind this charter was an act of piety and royal patronage to the Church. At this time the Fenland Abbey of Ramsay was extremely wealthy and powerful, owning vast sheep runs, and having one of the best business organisations in the country. To win greater fame for the abbey, the abbot secured the remains of Saint Ives, a famous martyr, and had them transferred to Huntingdonshire. The gift of the fair was intended to celebrate the creation of the new shrine, and to provide revenue for its upkeep. St Ives Fair quickly became an important centre of trade. Much of this early success can be attributed to the business acumen of the abbots of Ramsey, but the site was ideally suited to prosper. To the east was East Anglia, where, although it had not yet the pre-eminence to be achieved later, the cloth industry was beginning to prosper.* To the west were the rich grazing grounds, which, stretching across to the Welsh borders, provided the best quality wool in the whole of Europe. St Ives was the natural meeting ground for the East Anglian clothiers and the border graziers. Well served by roads and rivers, it was small wonder that the fair soon became one of the largest in the country.

Some thirty years later Henry I gave a charter for another fair which was to become as famous, and even more notorious, than St Ives. The story behind the foundation of Saint Bartholomew's Fair in London was unusual, if not unique, in the history of fairs. Shortly before the king's own death his favourite jester, Rahere, fell seriously ill, and vowed that if he should recover he would become a monk. Rahere did recover, and true to his oath asked the king to give him a piece of land on which to build a monastery. Henry granted him a plot and messuage in Smithfield on which Rahere built his monastery dedicated to St Bartholomew. Unfortunately the ex-jester found the upkeep and management of the foundation more difficult than expected, and within a few years the monastery was virtually destitute. Once again he appealed to the king, and in 1135 was granted the right to hold a fair on the land adjacent to the monastery, and to use its revenue for the upkeep of St Bartholomew's. Thus was created London's most famous fair, which was to prove one of the most durable of the medieval charters. Being in the capital it was always well attended and so great was its popularity that St Bartholomew's was soon renowned for rioting and immorality. It was, however, situated near the royal court, and was frequently visited by the king and courtiers, so that little was done to check its free-licence.

It was almost a century later when another fair dedicated to St Bartholomew was founded. In 1211, King John gave a charter to the leper hospital of St Mary Magdalene in Cambridge allowing a fair to be held in the nearby fields at Stourbridge, its revenue to be devoted to the welfare of its inmates. Local legend had it that this charter merely confirmed a fair which had been started almost a thousand years before by a Roman admiral, who had seized

*See *Wool: East Anglia's Golden Fleece.*

control of Britain for a short time in the third century. The truth of this is impossible to decide, but certainly the fair was an immediate success. Ideally situated to benefit from the rising importance of the East Anglian cloth industry, and well served by Roman roads, particularly the Icknield Way, Stourbridge Fair began to attract merchants from all over Europe. It began to flourish at a time when the older towns and the fairs associated with them had begun their steep decline, and certainly the lack of guild control was a great attraction. One sign of this success was that the hospital of St Mary Magdalene soon lost control of the fair, ownership becoming a question of bitter dispute between the Cambridge colleges and the town authorities. Although until the Reformation the colleges secured the revenues of the fair, the fairground was frequently a battle ground between the 'Town' and 'Gown'. A surer sign of the success of Stourbridge Fair was its effect upon its older neighbour at St Ives. Many merchants began to desert St Ives in favour of the new fair, so that Stourbridge soon became a rival, and quickly surpassed and eclipsed its counterpart.

With the development of these and other English fairs, the town and its close parochialism ceased to control the nation's trade. The fair, not the town, was to be the main avenue of European trade. Although hampered by a shortage of currency, despite the increase in bullion through the Levant trade, the amount of international commerce expanded steadily throughout the remainder of the Middle Ages. Control of this trade was not to remain exclusively with the fairs, because they were liable to disruption through the frequent wars of the period. The main rival to the fair was the regulated company, which, with its international interests and great power, was able to manipulate trade to a much greater extent than the patrons of a fair. For three hundred years the fair was to be one of the great features of medieval civilisation, until it in its turn was supplanted by forces which were to alter the direction of European history.

The Fairground

THE responsibility for organising a fair rested with the patron, whether nobleman, bishop, abbot, or Town Council. At first this was no more difficult than the preparation for a normal market, because the early fairs seldom lasted for more than three days. By the High Middle Ages the duration of the fair had been increased by additional charters. Few of the major fairs lasted less than a fortnight. Indeed at one stage the St Giles Fair at Winchester had charters allowing it to last for twenty-four days, although subsequently it was reduced to sixteen days. By the fourteenth century St Ives Fair at the height of its prosperity spread over forty days. Consequently the amount of preparation to ensure the smooth running of events of this duration was obviously considerable.

The preparatory work fell into several categories. One of the first considerations was the problem of coping with the vast crowds. This in itself was a twofold matter. People had to be encouraged to come and provided with accommodation once they had arrived. Although fairs were independent of the towns, it was important that the fairground should be sited close to a town so that the more important visitors had the opportunity to lodge in comfort at a castle, monastery, or inn. A large proportion of the general public had no hope of such comfort, and came prepared to sleep out in the fields and woods, but as they were used to a hard life camping would not be too onerous for them during the summer months. Even though it was necessary to make sure that there was land for the people to camp on, accommodation was not such a severe problem as might be expected. Of equal importance was the question of feeding the crowds which would be in the neighbourhood for several weeks. For the most part the local tradesmen, who regarded these extra sales as part of their profit from the fair, could be relied upon to buy in sufficient supplies. Even so it was incumbent upon the patron and his officials to make certain that there was enough food for all the people and animals, so that there were no sudden shortages and crises. This often meant that the patron bought up supplies and stored them in his manorial barns, and then sold them at advantageous prices.

The preparation of the fairground itself had to be started well in advance. For this purpose the patron had to hire a large number of temporary labourers and officials to supplement his normal retinue. A prime necessity was to keep the approach roads in a state of good repair. During the winter months all medieval roads deteriorated, and the traffic of the early spring churned the surfaces into large ruts and potholes. Gangs of labourers were employed to fill in the potholes and level the roads with rubble, and then the last mile and entry to the fairground was finished off with gravel and sometimes cobbles. The site itself was cleared of any rubbish which had accumulated since the previous year, and the grass mown to a reasonable length.

After the rough labouring had been completed carpenters and maintenance men were called in to overhaul the fairground equipment. This was not the swings and roundabouts associated with today's fairs, but the stalls and permanent buildings used for trading. Many fairgrounds resembled a small town, because in the centre were groups of houses and booths which remained there all the year round. After the Reformation had led to the closure of the St Ives Fair the original houses of the new town of St Ives were the obsolete fair booths formerly belonging to the Abbot of Ramsey. All such booths belonged to a patron and were leased out to the highest bidders. The houses were better than ordinary booths because they provided sleeping quarters for the merchant and had plenty of storage space. All these had to be kept in repair as did the collapsible stalls which were hired out to the less wealthy traders. All the warehouses and storage sheds had to be repaired and cleaned out. Once the running repairs had been carried out, officials had to inspect the whole site to decide the general lay-out for the fair. More workmen then moved in to erect the stalls, construct the pens for livestock, and build the show rings for displaying the animals. It was then time to prepare areas for games and competitions, and build the raised seats and pavilions for the use of the nobility and gentry.

While this army of workmen were transforming the fairground the patron and his officials were busily working out the intricate affairs of the organisation. Much of this consisted in the receipt of advanced bookings, and the allotment of stallage to merchants.

This was important as it was necessary to know how many stall-holders were likely to be present, and what crafts and trades they represented. Such calculations had to be made at a reasonably early stage, because the fair, like the market, was divided up into quarters segregating the rival crafts. Consequently the proportions of the various parts of the fairground had to be decided before the workmen erected the temporary stalls. This side of affairs was not so difficult as might appear at first sight because with the popular fairs the same people would return year after year; much of the work would consist of confirming return bookings. The booking of stallage represented part of the assured income of the patron, and as prices remained relatively static during the Middle Ages accounting would not be difficult. Against this small percentage of advance income had to be set the considerable outlay of providing entertainment. Much of the entertainment of the fair was spontaneous, being provided by the troupes of wandering players who spent the summer months travelling from fair to fair for the money they would earn from the crowds of visitors. In the same way there was no difficulty in attracting knights and athletes of high reputation to take part in the sports and competitions. On the other hand the reputation of the fair, and the patron, rested upon the high quality of these events, and of the prizes distributed to the winners.

A large part of the revenue accruing from the fair came from the tolls and taxes listed in the charter. Often the patron had the right to take all the profits of fines levied in the fair court. Sometimes, however, the king kept the court in his own hands, or only allowed the patron a share of the profits. This necessitated the employment of a large number of temporary clerks and officers to collect these dues. Toll houses had to be put up on all the approach roads to the fairground, and these had to be manned well in advance because many people would begin to arrive at least a week before the official opening. At the same time a special court had to be convened to settle any disputes which might arise over the collection of tolls. This situation arose because of the counterclaims over the right to levy toll and the exemption from tax. Many of the local merchants belonging to the Gild Merchant, or more powerful craft guilds, had freedom from dues written into their town charters. Such claims were settled reasonably easily because most of the temporary officials were local residents, who were well versed in the laws of the district. More difficult were the cases brought by visiting merchants, who had bought, or been given, a general clearance from all local tolls. Such cases had to be scrutinised carefully and set against the rights of the patron. Fortunately the court had a clear ruling in such cases, and the whole matter depended upon the date of the rival grants: the older charter always taking precedence. Apart from charging tolls on the people coming into the fairground the officials had to collect tariffs on all the goods brought to the fair. This in itself was often difficult, although there was a fixed scale of charges ranging from ¼d. to 1s. The problem here was not caused by complex legal claims, but by the astuteness of the carriers, who were very adroit in concealing the true nature of their goods.

At the same time the roads and fairground had to be policed by the local ward constables, and men at arms from the patron's own retinue. Much of this work was normal traffic control, but all arrivals had to be carefully scrutinised because although normal criminals were safe from arrest, efforts were always made to apprehend any outlaws, who were then handed over to the nearest sheriff. A close watch was kept upon the well known troublemakers so that they could be kept under surveillance to prevent riots and brawls before they could become serious. This police work was complicated by the arrival of pilgrims coming to participate in the Church Festival, which usually coincided with the beginning of the fair, especially as many of the pilgrims intended to stay to visit the fair. The difficulty of the over-worked officials was increased by the presence of the many clergymen coming to the festival. Although the Catholic Church recognised the commercial value of the fair, and Pope Hadrian IV had issued a degree blessing all fairs, the fairground was generally thought to be unsuitable for the clergy. This meant that clerics were forbidden to attend fairs, and often officials had the additional task of keeping a look-out for younger clergymen, who were tempted to savour the wordly delights of the fairground.

It was necessary for the patron and his officers to engage in some adroit public relations with local representatives of the Church and Town. At first sight this would appear to be an easy task as the patron himself was often a high Church dignitary, and his officials drawn from the principal burgesses of the town. In fact the position was not so easy as, frequently there was, emnity between clergy and laity. Thus it was often difficult to create good will between all the conflicting interests. As the success of the whole fair depended upon the full co-operation of all concerned it was essential to resolve these differences. In many cases the beginning of a fair coincided with a religious festival and it was important that the two events should be properly synchronised so that the one complemented the other. Dignitaries from the Church, the local nobility and the town would all be present at the festival, and if the right atmosphere was achieved they would all play their role in the ensuing fair. It was not only the local dignitaries who had to be propitiated, as it was equally desirable to have the good-will of the guilds. Although the guilds exercised no authority over the fair their full participation was a considerable boost to trade. Moreover the guilds were responsible for performing the cycle of Mystery Plays, which formed part of the more important Church Feasts. These pageants were extremely popular and were sure to attract large crowds, and it was a considerable asset to a fair if one of these cycle of plays formed part of the entertainment.

Another aspect of the fair which had to be settled in advance was the question of pre-emption. Just as at the market the Crown wrote into the original charter a clause preserving the royal right to have first choice of any goods offered for sale at the fair. Indeed as the fair provided the opportunity to buy in bulk at wholesale prices such rights were more important than at any other time. Following the Crown the patron and officials had the second choice of goods, but it was open to other people to purchase the right of pre-emption from the patron. As mentioned earlier, it was normal for all the monastic houses and castles in the neighbourhood, which had to cater for large households, to hold these licenses. As a large proportion of goods sold at the fair were raw materials for specific crafts the local guilds were eager to share this privilege. In the later Middle Ages the great regulated companies, such as the Hanseatic League, bought rights of pre-emption to help in their control of certain commodities. Basically all these claims, like those over the collection of tolls, should have been decided upon the date of the grant. Such decisions rested with the Clerk of the Fair, but frequently the matter rested upon the power and influence of the claimant.

Like any other large public event an enormous amount of advance planning had to go into the staging of a fair. Although much of the preparation was routine, the patron had to fear comparisons with previous fairs and rival events. The organisers could not afford to let the standards drop for fear that the attendance would fall. Each fair had to be kept up to a peak, and every year some new and exotic attraction had to be staged to maintain the public interest. Perhaps the most difficult part of the management was the sheer length of the great fairs. The programme for each day had to be arranged to maintain appeal, and the star attractions had to be carefully spaced to keep the crowds coming for the duration of the fair.

THE last few days before the opening of the fair were ones of mounting excitement as the crowds flocked into the neighbourhood, and the traders made their last minute arrangements. The final stage was the proclaiming of the fair. Normal business virtually came to a stop for several miles around and trade was limited to the sale of foodstuffs, the ordinary law courts were suspended, and work on the farms was reduced to a bare minimum. The actual proclamation had to be made on each of the three, or four, days before the official opening. The Town Criers accompanied by the Waits would announce the forthcoming event from traditional points in the town and around the fairground. In some cases these ceremonies took the form of processions in full livery, which added to the atmosphere of the occasion. On the days of the proclamation the tempo of life in the whole neighbourhood slowed down in anticipation of the official opening.

Often the actual opening of the fair took place after the celebration of Mass in the cathedral, or main church of the town. All the local dignitaries would attend the service in their full regalia, and would then go to the Guild Hall. In many cases this was the moment when authority was handed over to the Clerk of the Fair and his officials, and for the duration of the fair they would supersede the normal town officers and local officials. Then led by the patron they would go in procession to the fairground, the Town Waits and all the guildsmen in full livery. At the entrance to fairground the patron mounted a rostrum to make his speech of welcome to all the visitors, expressing the hope that all trading would be conducted honestly, and that everyone would behave in a Christian and fitting manner. Then the fair was declared open, either by ringing a bell, or hoisting a large leather glove on the end of a long pole.

Each day trading lasted from 10 a.m. until sunset, and no dealing could take place except between these times. It was customary to set aside certain days for specialised trading. This was often true of livestock sales. For convenience the show rings were sited on the outskirts of the fairground, or sometimes in a separate enclosure. In any case it was necessary to make the streets between the blocks of stalls and booths quite wide to allow freedom of access for animals. Some fairs had a special reputation for the sale of livestock, such as the Nottingham Goose Fair, the Hull Horse Fair and, at a later date, the Yarmouth Herring Fair. Every fair, however, had its livestock section which was very important for the local landowners and farmers, setting prices for the remainder of the year.

In these days of mechanised transport it is difficult to imagine the difficulties entailed in driving animals to the fairground. Yet animals were sent over long distances to be sold at the traditional fairs, and were reared specially for these events. Norfolk geese and hens were walked all the way to London and Nottingham. Border sheep and cattle were driven from the Scottish and Welsh marches to the southern fairs, and the London markets where they would fetch the best prices. This would take weeks along the old trackways and drove roads, where they would not obstruct the already congested main roads. The drovers had to make the journey in easy stages so as to keep the animals in the best condition. They would take with them, on packhorses, a supply of hurdles so that they could set up temporary pens each night, or for longer rest periods. Such long journeys even on the unmetalled roads would cripple the beasts unless special precautions were taken. Horses were shod, so that drovers only had to carry a supply of spare horseshoes, and a portable anvil to effect the necessary repairs. Cattle and sheep presented a more difficult problem, and they had to be shod with special leather boots to preserve their feet. Geese and hens were even more difficult to deal with, especially as their feet were particularly ill-suited to long journeys. The normal method found to overcome this problem was to walk them through a shallow pool of pitch, and then across a bed of course sand. Here again the drovers had to take a supply of pitch and sand with them so that they could renew the coating at intervals.

Even with all these precautions the animals were usually in poor condition by the time they arrived at their destination. For this reason they had to be brought to the vicinity of the fair, or market, several weeks before they were to be sold, so that they could be fattened-up. Providing pasture for these drovers was part of the preliminary work of the Clerk of the Fair. Local farmers hired out fields for this purpose. Sometimes the drovers kept the beasts until they were sold at the fair, but frequently they were bought by dealers, who kept them for the weeks needed to bring them back into condition and then re-sold them. This was often necessary because fair law insisted that in all sales of livestock both seller and buyer had to be known to the Clerk of the Fair, or his subordinates. On the day of the sale the animals had to be driven into the enclosures before the day's business opened, and then each beast had to be paraded for a period of time up to an hour.

Apart from being the major event in the farming calender, in that they set prices in other ways, fairs were very important to the farming community. They were able to meet their fellows from all over the locality, and from further afield, and could exchange all the news and the latest ideas and farming. During such discussions conditions and wages of work for the labourers would be fixed to maintain a uniform level. Many farmers kept diaries showing a table of prices, the best time of the year to buy and sell, and which were the fairs and markets to attend to sell specific commodities. In days when all the labourers were illiterate, and many of the farmers were scarcely any better, the fair was an essential landmark in the farming year: an occasion which came at a fixed time and was remembered by all those who were present. It was ideal for the making of contracts, particularly as there were plenty of witnesses, which was the main consideration in medieval law. Indeed many fairs were recognised as hiring fairs. This was a good arrangement as all concerned knew that the beginning of the fair terminated the contract, and so there could be no disputes. Michaelmas was the usual time for making these contracts with the labourers, this is the reason why many farming dates still run from this time of the year. Apart from hiring labourers the farmers had the opportunity to meet their colleagues to confirm rents, leases and other business deals, which would then run for the next twelve months.

This side of the fair, however, only formed a minute part of the real business. The main part of the fairground was divided into sectors in which almost every facet of medieval commerce and industry were represented. Generally each section was reserved for vendors of the same trade, or craft. At Stourbridge Fair, for instance, the large central area was called the Duddery, because only cloth and clothing were on sale there. It was among the streets of stalls that the heart of the fair —the wholesale trade— was to be found, which kept the commerce of the Western world circulating year by year. To a large extent it represented the bulk of the patron's revenue. All buying and selling was subject to toll, the parties involved in each deal having to pay the sum of 1d. to the fair officers. In addition the goods sold were subject to a sliding scale of charges depending on the quality and quantity. To a large section of the crowds, however, the general dealing in small articles attracted the greatest attention. Merchandise from all over the known world could be found displayed on the stalls, and merchants from Arabia and Africa mingled with those from Iceland and the wild Slavonic lands of eastern Germany. Many people came merely to see these exotic strangers and their fabulous merchandise.

Predominate among these foreign merchants were the Italians, who continued to hold a major place in English commerce until the fourteenth century. Every year fleets of Italian ships came to the major English ports laden with the luxuries of the Levant trade. These goods were stored in the warehouses belonging to the Italian factories. For their return voyage the ships were loaded with the foodstuffs and raw materials bought by the Italian English agents during the preceding twelve months. Although some of this merchandise was sold directly to English trading concerns, a large proportion was distributed through the fairs.

The wide distribution of luxury goods from the Mediterranean made possible by the fair was to have an important effect upon the development of industry and civilisation in England. Displayed on the stalls at the fair were the silks, satins, cottons, jewellery, spices, glassware and carpets, which were otherwise unobtainable to the normal English buyer. In the main it was the nobles and wealthy middle classes who bought the luxury goods, but yeoman and peasant could purchase some of the myriad of smaller articles, such as the ribbons and trinkets which were on sale. For the Italians this was only a fraction of their normal trade, but it was the means by which the standard of living and level of civilisation rose in England. At the same time manufacturers all over the country began to copy the quality and style of the Mediterranean goods, and gradually a native luxury trade developed.

The merchants from other countries came to the English fairs with goods which had proved to have popular appeal, or were otherwise unobtainable in England. From the kingdoms of northern Spain came wine merchants selling the percursors of the modern ports and sherries. Southern Spain was still controlled by the Moorish kings, but Arab traders came to sell the famous swords and armour from Toledo, fine silver work and damasks. Visiting French merchants were not particularly interested in selling wine, because there was a tremendous annual turnover in wine from the English territories in Guienne. Instead they carried with them the mirrors, glassware, silks and furniture, in the manufacture of which the French were much more skilled than their English counterparts. From Flanders came the famed tapestries of Arras, and a wide variety of brass and copperware. Men from Iceland came to England to sell their cured fish and bone carvings. From the Baltic and eastern Germany the descendants of the Vikings brought rich furs, honey, wax, hemp and amber. Amongst this wealth of the more normal merchandise were to be found stalls selling caged song birds, monkeys, parrots and a wide variety of hunting dogs. A strange sight to modern eyes were the stalls of the relic sellers who offered splinters from the true Cross, a stone thrown at Sebastian, an arrow head from the body of St Edmund, and a host of other amulets.

Herein lay all the superficial glitter of the fair, the sights and sounds of which formed the basis of conversation for the next year. The real business of the fair was carried out by small groups of businessmen, who shunned the tinsel glitter and the flamboyance of the main fairground, but made deals which sometimes equalled the entire royal revenue. As in the case of the farmers these men found the fair a convenient time to renew their contacts, and to make or reaffirm, commercial deals with colleagues from all over Western Europe. One of the main impediments to commerce was the ever-present shortage of currency. Consequently credit facilities were of the greatest importance, and the fair fulfilled this essential need. Not until the seventeenth century was the country to have the advantage of a true banking system, when William III, in 1694, founded the Bank of England. Until that time loans had to be obtained from wealthy merchant families, or credit terms had to be arranged between business contacts. The fair was the one time of the year when financial arrangements could be discussed, and credit terms made for the following year. By this means English merchants were able to ensure that they would be able to trade freely on the Continent without financial crises. With the growth of the great regulated companies these considerations became less vital, and from this point the fairs began to decline. Until then personal contact had been an essential ingredient of medieval trade, giving the opportunity to discuss market trends and conditions in other countries. For the individual merchant such information was invaluable, when advance warning of a possible outbreak of war, or change of government would make all the difference to the peaceful conditions needed for commerce.

These multifarious activities were under the jurisdiction of the Clerk of the Fair and his officials, who had replaced the normal magistrates for the duration of the fair. He was responsible for enforcing and interpretating the Law Merchant as it was applied to the fair. In many respects this was similar to the normal laws governing the market, but there were some important variations. The Clerk would have at his disposal the normal law enforcement officers, the Common Sergeant and the Ward Constables. As the fair was noted for unruliness the patron generally placed a detachment of his men-at-arms at the Clerk's disposal to help maintain order. During the fair it was usual for a special court to be held in readiness to hear any criminal charges that might arise. In most cases the magistrates would merely decide whether the Sergeant had presented a valid case, and then send the offenders to languish in the town gaol until the next Assize. In minor cases such as pickpockets and cutpurses, the magistrates often handed out summary sentences.

This aspect of law enforcement was routine, but most of the fair patrons had obtained royal charters allowing them to hold their own special court, which dealt with commercial cases. Generally this was known as the Court of Pie Powder, which was a corruption of the French, 'pieds poudreux'. The term means literally the court of dusty feet, referring to the fact it dealt with merchants who had travelled, and as the roads were notoriously dusty during the summer they would be covered in dust. As a large proportion of the people attending the fair had come long distances specially for the occasion and would be leaving at the end of the fair, it was essential that there should be no undue delay in deciding all the cases which arose. Consequently the Court of Pie Powder superseded all other courts, and had the right to deal summarily with all cases without having to refer cases to the county assize. In most cases all the profits arising from fines passed to the patron as part of his perquisites. Similarly the commercial Assizes of Bread and Ale, and Weights and Measures were combined in the Court of Pie Powder.

The Law Merchant was by no means uniform, and each town had its own interpretations and variation. Frequently the variations were designed to benefit the resident, and placed the 'foreign' merchant at a disadvantage. This was obviously impractical at fairs where the foreigner was predominate, and so in time the Law Merchant used at fairs was made uniform throughout Europe and had no bias. In all cases between freemen and 'foreigners' the jury in court had to be made up of equal numbers of local men and visitors. Disputes had to be heard continuously hour by hour, and all fines and settlements were made within 'three ebbs and floods'. Pleas could not be prolonged for more than twenty-four hours, because this would delay the workings of the court. In cases involving a merchant sueing a seaman, or any other specialist, there had to be counsels, who were expert in the aspect of law in question, present in the court to advise the contestants. All those concerned with a case were allowed to speak freely without prejudice. Any party could engage a Sergeant at Law to speak for them, but this was always regarded as sharp practice, and the magistrates were more likely to find for those who presented their own case. If the magistrates considered that either defendant, or plaintiff, put forward a poor case through ignorance of the law, they were given the chance to present their case again after expert advice. It was possible to appeal against a decision of the court, but the appeal had to be made immediately, or it was over-ruled as invalid. If any of the jurors were found guilty of accepting bribes, they were fined ten times the amount of the original fine imposed on the guilty person.

The vast majority of the cases heard in the Court of Pie Powder resulted from direct actions between two merchants, accusations of selling short, or inferior measure, and of fore-stalling, or regrating. For this reason there was a duplicate set of weights and measures, one kept in the courtroom, and the other in charge of the Clerk, or the Common Sergeant. For convenience the measures were sited near the centre of the fairground, where they were accessible to all disputants. The spot was often marked by a central cross similar to those found in the town marketplaces. This would take the form of a standing cross, or a small building where the officials could sit while they were waiting. The collection of weights and measures was impressive and varied, as each trade and craft had its own type of measure. Thus could be found a 'potele', a 'quarte', a 'pynte', and a 'gille' of pewter for dry measure; 'panyers', 'hopirs', 'moduses', and 'firtiendels' for general measures; a 'peck' and '½ peck' for small measure; and finally a 'gallon', a 'potell', a 'third part', and a 'quartt' of wood to measure ale. Disputants would first go to the cross where their measures were checked, and if any discrepancy was found the parties would go to court, where the case would be heard and the measures rechecked. In cases of disputed quality the parties were taken to the court, where the goods were tested by the assize, to discover whether ale had been salted and watered, or if cloth had been stretched, or dry calendered.

In most cases the guilty parties were fined, but other punishments were given, and these formed part of the amusement for the visitors to the fair. Brewers who were found to have sold bad beer were ducked in a convenient pond in a ducking stool. Bakers found to have sold short measure, or bad bread, were drawn round the fairground on a sledge with one of their loaves tied round their necks so that people could throw rubbish at them. There were the stocks and pillory which were set up in a prominent position, and any minor offenders were locked in them until nightfall. Cutpurses and pickpockets were often punished in this manner, but if they were second offenders they had one ear cut off. Anyone found guilty of selling, or receiving, stolen goods was expelled from the fairground, having to pay double the value of the goods to the rightful owner, and forfeiting the remainder of his goods to the patron. Apprentices and servants were not punished by the court if they misbehaved, because it was held that their masters were responsible for them, and it was their duty to chastise the offenders. In general people were given a great deal of license during the fair, but the crime of sacrilege was always treated harshly, and any offenders were branded on the forehead.

Amusements

ALTHOUGH the main function of the fair was to provide a
centre for trade, it had a very important lighter purpose. A
fair was the great local holiday event for the countryside, and was
a means of releasing the high spirits of people who had to live a
restricted existence for most of the year. It acted as a safety valve
for people who were never far removed from violence. The
sports and contests provided at a fair were a peaceful means of
relieving these inhibitions, while the entertainments maintained
a light-hearted atmosphere, which lessened the likelihood of
violence. For this reason there was a tremendous variety of
entertainments, but very few of them are to be seen on a
modern fairground. Life was much harsher in the Middle Ages,
and the entertainments enjoyed by the people were much more
boisterous and bloodthirsty.

The first day of the fair provided the most decorous
entertainment. The ecclesiastical ceremonies with processions
to the church or cathedral, followed by the formal opening of
the fairground provided a spectacle for the crowds of visitors.
For most people normal life was very drab and monotonous, so
they loved to see processions displaying the rich robes of the
dignitaries, and the liveries of the guildsmen. Frequently the
guilds began the round of entertainments. These, it is true, were
connected more with the celebration of the Church Festival
than with the fair, but they provided a great attraction at the
beginning of the holiday. In many towns the guilds marked
important Feast Days by staging a Cycle of Mystery Plays
depicting scenes from the Old Testament. The plays themselves
were performed on stages erected on large waggons, which
could be drawn to stopping places along a prearranged route.
Each guild produced their own play, which often had some
connection with their trade, or was a pun of their craft. Thus the
story of Jonah and the Whale was acted by the Seamens' Guild.
These plays had an important educational purpose in an age when
the majority of people were illiterate and helped them to understand the stories in the Bible. The performance of a whole cycle

of these plays would take the entire day. They were popular, particularly as the stories were well-known. Although the standard of acting was not usually very high, the entertainment came from comic by-play and use of dialect.

On the fairground itself the patron provided large scale amusements, which were timed carefully to maintain interest among the crowds. One of the most popular entertainments of the Middle Ages was the tournament, which was sure to draw great crowds of spectators. The medieval jousting was the result of the nobility's insatiable love of fighting. In times of peace the only thing to relieve the tedium, apart from hunting and hawking, was to organise mock battles, or jousts. Originally these had been actual miniature battles, but by the fourteenth century tournaments had their own intricate rules, and were fought with blunted weapons. It depended upon the influence and standing of the patron as to how splendid an event he could stage. The attraction and popularity of a jousting match depended upon the fame and quality of the knights who took part. Once the reputation of a tournament had been established knights and champions from all over Europe would come to take part. The actual arena would be set up adjacent to the fairground. The lists themselves were lined with covered stands where visiting nobles and the gentry could sit to watch the contests. Pavilions were erected for the knights, where the squires and attendants armed their masters. The jousts were run either between single contestants, or small groups of knights. Thus the gentlemen of Cambridgeshire might hold the lists against knights from other counties. This spectacle would be held over a number of days, and the prizes would be distributed on the last day of the fair.

While the glamour of the tournament created enormous interest, the majority of the people at the fair came from the middle and lower classes, and a great gulf existed between them and the nobility. To meet the needs of this larger audience the patron provided other contests in which they could participate more fully. At a time when the English long bow was the terror of the battlefields of Europe, archery was an extremely popular pastime throughout England. Indeed during the reign of Edward III it was forbidden to play dangerous games such as football because it wasted time which should be spent in practising at the archery butts. This produced a very high proficiency, so that men from any class could become skilled bowmen. For this reason the great archery contests held at the fairs attracted large entries, and great interest. Master bowmen from every part of the country would come to test their skill, and add to their reputations. In an age when regional and local loyalties were very strong, there was considerable rivalry between the bowmen of the shires. This added to the popularity of the archery contests at the fair, because visitors had the opportunity to cheer on their local champions. These competitions were carefully arranged to test all the skills of archery. Long and short butts, garlands, wands, roving and long shots enabled the bowmen to show skill, strength and quickness of reaction and eye. Archery bouts were one of the greatest attractions for the fairgoer, and were protracted for the duration of the fair, coming to a climax with the presentation of prizes on the final day.

For the less skilful a number of other sporting contests were held, which provided a great amount of amusement for competitors and spectators alike. Quarterstaff bouts, the yeoman's equivalent to the swordplay of the nobles and gentry, were popular, and involved a considerable amount of skill. Wrestling offered a wide variety of styles, as each region had developed its form of the sport, and this offered the visitors the opportunity of following the fortunes of their own champions. Another sport which was taken from the formal military training of squires was tilting at the quintain. This often took two forms: its original purpose was to train horsemen to use a lance. A pivoted board was attached to the top of a post, and the object was to strike one end of the board with the lance, but avoid the other end swinging round and hitting the rider. At the fair a man with a pole 'rode' on the shoulders of his partner, who often did his utmost to hinder his rider. An alternative form of the sport took place on a convenient pond, the jouster standing in a punt and tilting at the quintain set in the middle of the water. Other forms of this competition were jousting at the ring, or the sandbag. More familiar country sports, such as climbing or walking the slippery pole, and wrestling for the pig, were provided throughout the duration of the fair. The provision and variety of these competitions, and the quantity of prizes, did much to make, or mar, the reputation of the fair with the country people.

Another manner in which the crowds were kept amused was by watching a variety of bloodsports. Arenas, pits and enclosures were leased to sponsors for the length of the fair and these men staged a whole series of events, charging the entrants and spectators for the use of the facilities. To the majority of people bull fighting is always associated with Spain, but during the Middle Ages varieties of the sport were much more widely distributed. Most large towns had their own bullrings, although in England the sport was more akin to the milder version to be found in the south of France, than the modern Spanish national pastime. It was more usual to find bull baiting at the fairs. Several breeds of dog were used to bait the bulls, but the mastiff was the most popular. Generally three or four dogs were set upon a bull at the same time, and it was quite common for the dogs to lose the contest.

Bear baiting was very similar. The bears were imported from the Continent, and were in charge of bearwards, who had to hold a license. It was a common sight to see the bears being led along the roads from one town, or fair to the next on the itinerary. During these journeys the bears were securely muzzled as they were dangerous, and might have become infuriated if worried by stray mongrels. The bearward was held responsible for any incidents that might occur, and had to make sure the beast was properly secured every night. During the actual baiting the bears were unmuzzled, and care was taken that they were not seriously injured because they were such valuable animals. Not all the bears seen at the fairs were used for baiting, but were trained to entertain in much the same manner as circus animals today. The performing bears were a very popular side show, as they danced to music, and carried out various well-rehearsed tricks.

By the end of the Middle Ages bull and bear baiting had become unfashionable, and the sport tended to die out. Other types of animal sports, however, continued to be popular until the nineteenth century. Cock fighting had not become the 'rage' with the *haut ton* which it was to be in the eighteenth century, but it had a wide following. The contests were fought in a small, specially constructed ring, which gave the backers a clear view of the battle. The cocks were carefully bred, and had particularly powerful fighting spurs. Each bird had its trainer and handler, and was brought to the ring in a bag, and only slipped out at the beginning of the bout. Each part of the country had its own breed of fighting cock, all of which had their supporters. The bouts, themselves, were bloody affairs, which frequently ended with the death of one, or both cocks. Such blood sports, while they were an important attraction, had a relatively limited appeal, although they had the solid support of the *aficionado*.

Of more universal appeal were the entertainers on the fair-ground. These were the mountebanks and strolling players, who were to be immortalised later in the playhouses of the Elizabethan era. Their descendents can still be found in many branches of entertainment today. The folk singers are but an up to date personification of the strolling minstrel, who sang of the romantic deeds of an age of chivalry. The jugglers, tumblers and acrobats can still be found in many places, including the ring of the professional wrestler. During the Middle Ages the term strolling player was particularly apt, for these entertainers did literally stroll from one place of recreation to the next. Not for them the security of a long run with full bookings, or even the comparative safety of the provincial tour. They were constantly on the move, never being quite sure where their next meal and bed would be found. For all except the winter months they tramped the roads, moving from town to castle, hoping that they would be given lodging for the performance which they gave. Their wanderings were not aimless, for they, like the merchants, planned their routes to coincide with the cycle of fairs, knowing that they would be sure of good takings. The players were landless and masterless men, who in the eyes of the authorities were no better than beggars and outlaws. Men who knew that they had to earn enough money during the summer season to be able to afford a lodging for the winter when the roads were impassable. Yet like the men of the hanses, they had their own fraternity, and for them the fair was a place to meet old friends and renew contacts.

The tumblers, jugglers and fire-eaters were very closely associated with the minstrels, and formed part of the fraternity. Their appearance has been made very familiar from the jokers in a pack of playing cards, with the parti-coloured hose, fool's cap and bells. The more fortunate performers found themselves safe posts as jesters at the Court, or in one of the great baronial halls. Several, such as Rahere, rose to high positions under royal favour. Often such men were dwarfs, or had some deformity, but they were highly intelligent and acted as advisors, or spies for their masters. Others spent their lives wandering all over Europe entertaining at castles and manor houses, learning new tricks and turns in the countries through which they passed. These people were skilled and artful performers, who changed their acts to suit the audiences before which they were appearing. Their turns, apart from the straightforward fire-eating, sword swallowing and juggling, were a blend of acrobatics and music. Although the tumblers were uneducated men, many of them had a very good musical ear, and could play several instruments. They normally formed themselves into small groups of three, or four, each member having his own especial repertoire. The performance was accompanied on a variety of instruments, each member of the troupe being able to leap down at the end of his own turn, pick up another instrument, and carry on the music without a break. Some of the more skilled could contrive to carry on their tumbling and acrobatics, and play their instruments at the same time. Even when walking on their hands they would be playing a wind instrument, and have bells and tambourines fastened to their ankles so that they could continue the music.

Another group of well-known entertainers were the mummers. They are commemorated in the well known phrase 'dressed like a mummer at the fair'. This refers to the elaborate, and sometimes fantastic costume worn by the mummers, but it must be remembered that it was part of the stock in trade of all the entertainers to wear very showy, if tawdry, dress. To a certain extent the mummers were a secular counterpart to the guildsmen performing their mystery plays. In many ways they were like the minstrels, their folk plays recalling old legends and stories, which were part of popular lore. Themes such as St George and the Dragon, or the Crusader and the Turk, provoked patriotism and sentiment. At the same time such plays gave full rein for fantastic costume, swashbuckling, and comic duels. There were a variety of comic characters who, appeared in the most unlikely of settings, and flitted in and out of the almost non-existent plot. A great advantage of this type of play was that it could be adapted to fit any type of story, and the repertoire was often changed to suit the locality in which it was being performed. The characters were well known, and the onlookers had their own favourites, whose appearance was greeted with acclaim. A great deal depended upon the dialogue and mime, which was often in dialect, and contained local and topical gossip and jokes. The mummers' plays are still performed today, with characters such as St George, Father Christmas and other parts, some of them comic.

Another set-piece entertainment were the dancers. Today we tend to think of sword dancing and similar performances as being associated with Scotland and the north of England. During the Middle Ages there were traditional dances in every part of the country, which were widely known and appreciated. Although many of these still survive they are little publicised, and followed by a comparatively small number of interested spectators. Many of them were closely linked with the fairs because they dated back to pre-Christian times. Although this type of dance was usually performed on set days and at traditional ancient sites, the dancers often performed their ritual at the local fair. The dances themselves were pagan rites to mark the festivals of the old religion, but with the passing of the centuries they had come to form part of the nation's folk-lore. They were frequently a cross between mumming and a sword dance. The number of men who took part in the dance varied in different parts of the country. Each dance had its own traditional characters, the parts being handed down from father to son, so that a family would develop its own techniques for a particular character. Many of the dances had their grotesque beasts such as snap dragons, and hobby horses, which, again, were the responsibility of one family to maintain and animate. The dancers wore traditional costume, which sometimes resembled that of the morris dancers, but sometimes consisted of unwieldy hooped skirts, and masks. Once again mime and dialect played their part in the performance, but unlike the mummers, the dance had to follow its ritual quite closely, and there was less room for extemporisation. The climax came with the actual sword dance in which the chief dancer was dramatically 'beheaded' in a most realistic manner. This was a reminder of the forgotten pagan rite when the 'corn king' was sacrificed to bring fertility to the crops.

Another sight, which has become quite familiar because of its modern revival, was morris dancing. The origin of such dances is uncertain, but it is possible that they came from the Moslem Caliphate in Spain, morris being an anglicanisation of moorish, or morisco dances. During the Middle Ages morris dancing was widespread, and every locality had its own form of dance. The dancers had flamboyant costume with ribbons and bells, possibly supporting the Spanish origin. Each group was usually made up of six dancers, supported by a hobby horse and a 'fool'. The hobby horse consisted of a carved wooden horse's head, and a wide hooped skirt, or cloak. The 'fool' wore a many coloured costume, and carried a sheep's bladder balloon fastened to a stick. Both had to be good dancers, but their main task was to entertain the crowd, and hobby horse, in particular, had a reputation for flirting with all the pretty girls.* Another important part of a troupe was the musician who accompanied the dancers, usually on a pipe, drum, or fiddle. There were traditional dances from all parts of the country, although during the Middle Ages there was a strong association with the Robin Hood legend. The strongest centre of the morris dance was the Cotswolds, from whence most of the modern dance sequences are taken. Most of the dances from this area take the form of handkerchief, handclapping, or stick dances. From other parts of the Midlands came such variations as horn dances, in which reindeer antlers were carried, or processional dances which needed up to sixteen dancers. In the north the sword dancers were yet another variation. Unlike Scottish sword dances, the swords were carried and formed part of the dance. With long sword dancing there are a series of intricate steps which come to a climax with the formation of the swords into a star shaped 'lock'. Another form was the 'rapper' dance in which short swords were used. These dances very likely date back to pagan times, because the supporting characters have the names, 'king' and 'betty'. These refer back to the sacrifice of the corn king, and the betty was the man-woman cult figure of the old pagan religion. These dances were usually held at Whitsun, so that they were a great attraction at the Whit week fairs.

---

*From which the term ''horse play'' is derived.

II

The Decline of the Fair

DURING the fifteenth century the fairs underwent a steady and disastrous decline even in England, their main stronghold. The reasons for this were many and varied. Basically the fair had lost its position as the centre of international trade with the appearance of new methods of exchange in the later Middle Ages. The century saw a series of devastating wars during which the contacts, which were the lifeblood of the fair, were lost. At the same time a completely new vista of overseas commerce was beginning in which the traditional fair could no longer serve a useful part.

The first fundamental blow at the position of the fair was the creation of a new type of trading company during the fourteenth century. Control of European trade was slipping from the Italians, just as it had from the Jews. The native merchants of the northern countries were beginning to take control of their own affairs. Not having the financial resources accruing from the Levant trade at their disposal, they banded themselves into large companies for mutual benefit and support. One of the earliest of these regulated companies was the Merchant Staplers, into whose hands fell the fabulously lucrative English wool trade. The members of such a company traded as individuals, all abiding by the rules laid down by the governing committee, which was elected annually by the members. The advantage of this arrangement was that the combined influence and wealth of the members, backed by the grant of royal charters, made the company well able to exert wide influence, and compete on the Continent on equal terms with the Italians. The Staplers had their own 'mart' towns, both in England and on the Continent, and did not need to rely upon the fair as a means of distribution.

With the development of the English cloth industry the amount of wool available for export decreased, and so the influence of the Staplers waned. Their place, however, was soon taken by new companies, which grew to be wealthier and even more influential. The most famous of these were the Merchant Adventurers who operated from England, and the Hanseatic League with its centre around the Baltic. Like the Staplers these concerns had their own marketing methods, which largely by-passed the fairground. This meant that a large part of the European commerce was diverted from the fair which, in consequence, became less important. Moreover there was tremendous rivalry between the Hanse and the Adventurers, which did much to damage the old pattern of medieval trade. Both companies endeavoured to use any unscrupulous method to achieve their ends. This resulted in an increase in piracy, and commercial embargoes suddenly closed down markets. None of this was conducive to the freedom of international trade essential for the welfare of the fair.

At the same time there were other movements afoot prior to the fifteenth century, which worked to the detriment of the fair. The purpose of the chartered fairs had been to encourage trade at a time when Europe was backward, and conditions difficult for commerce. As the amount of contact with Italy and the more civilised countries of the Mediterranean increased, so the standard of living in the West improved. In every country industries were started, making it less essential to import manufactured goods from the Mediterranean. While demoting the status of the Italian merchant, this tended to have an adverse effect upon the fair. This meant that people no longer had to rely upon the fairground to buy luxury goods, because many of them could be purchased just as easily in any large town and, if the quality was slightly lower, so was the price. Consequently the fair was already in a weakened position before the changes of the next century completed their downfall.

Towards the end of the fourteenth century a new invader appeared in the Middle East following in the footsteps of the Huns and the Mongols. The Ottoman Turks quickly gained control of Asia Minor, and soon began to advance towards Constantinople, the key to the approaches of Europe. Despite a sudden and devastating Mongol raid under Tamerlain the Great, which almost destroyed the Ottoman Empire, the Turks recovered because the Christian nations were too busy quarrelling to take advantage of the situation. The westward advance was resumed, and Constantinople fell in 1453. The way was open for the Turks to launch an attack upon Europe: a menace which lasted until the seventeenth century. Of even greater immediate importance, the fall of Constantinople marked the end of the Middle Ages and the dawn of the modern period of history.

The effect of these changes had far reaching repercussions in the West. Throughout the Middle Ages Constantinople had been the cradle of Western civilisation, and after the seventh century, a bastion against the Moslem hordes. Alarmed by the successes of the Turks many Greek scholars fled to seek refuge in Italy, just as a thousand years previously Roman scholars fled to Greece to escape from the Goths. The Greeks brought not only their learning to Europe, but large collections of manuscripts containing the latest ideas of the Levant civilisations. Moreover they brought accurate manuscripts of the works of such great classical scholars as Aristotle, and Plato. In this manner the Renaissance began in Italy, and slowly spread to the remainder of Europe. Although the word renaissance suggests a revival of learning, in fact, it was the creation of a sophisticated European civilisation. Within this new society the fair came to play a minor economic rôle. At the same time the Renaissance undermined the old international values of the Middle Ages. The Pope and the Holy Roman Emperor were no longer regarded as the leaders of the West. New nation states in France, England, Portugal and Spain began to take over the leadership of Western Europe. This was another blow to the position of the fair, which depended upon the concept of internationalism, and with the appearance of national boundaries, the freedom of movement essential to the fairgoer was curtailed. Thereafter the fair ceased to be the centre of an international commerce.

The nation states had only achieved their position through a succession of bitter civil wars, as the new dynastic kings strove to overcome the power of the old feudal nobility. The fairs of the Champagne area had been the first to suffer from this development during the Hundred Years War, when the French kings had slowly driven the English out of their lands in France. The English nobles, with their battle-hardened retainers returned home, and then began to fight among themselves. The Wars of the Roses devastated England for a quarter of a century before Edward IV gained control of the country. Strangely enough the great fair flourished as never before, but it was a bright Indian summer, a harbinger of a bleak decline. With the death of Edward IV the wars restarted, and Henry Tudor triumphed at the battle of Bosworth in 1485. The coming of the Tudors ushered in the Renaissance, and an entirely new concept in the pattern of trade. The Wars of the Roses had robbed the English fairs of a large part of their trade, and they were in no position to meet this new challenge.

This was not the death of the English fairs, there had been disastrous wars before, and commerce had recovered. It was changes in the distant Mediterranean, and on even more faraway shores, which were irrevocably to end the fair as a commercial force. The cause of these changes was the conquests of the Ottoman Turks, who were fanatical Moslems and hated the Christians to such an extent that they refused to allow Westerners into their empire. With their control of the Levant they commanded the terminal ports of the overland route to India and the Far East. They were unwilling to allow the Italians to trade within their domain, and threatened to close down this trade route. Although this threat to sever the link between the West and the Levant was not enforced until the middle of the sixteenth century, it had a bad effect upon trade. Such uncertainty was detrimental to commerce, and men began to think of alternative routes to the Far East.

The Voyages of Discovery were not entirely the outcome of the need for new trade routes. Men such as Prince Henry of Portugal, nicknamed the 'navigator', took a tremendous interest in the ideas sparked off by the Renaissance, and this, combined with improvements in marine technology, made the voyages possible. At the beginning of the fifteenth century the Portuguese began to explore the western coastline of Africa, and by 1498 Vasco da Gama had reached the Indian port of Calicut. Six years previously he pioneered a western route to Asia across the Atlantic, reaching the West Indies and eventually the mainland of South America. Suddenly the Mediterranean was no longer the centre of the Western commercial world, and the Indians ceased to be the middlemen of the luxury trade. This caused a complete revolution in European commerce, as the ancient trade routes, which had been in use for several thousand years, were suddenly by-passed. The fairs, which had grown up as a natural outcome of this pattern of communication, became backwaters.

To cope with the new conditions, marketing methods had to be changed. Individual merchants could no longer afford to take all the risks involved in the long voyages to India and America. Whereas previously the longest voyages in European trade had only lasted for a few weeks, and the capital returns were quickly realised, expeditions to the New World could take over a year. No merchant could allow his capital to be tied up for so long, and a new form of trading company was created. A number of merchants would pool part of their capital to finance a trading venture, and would then share the profits in proportion to the amount they had contributed. At first these joint stock companies were only temporary associations, but as they were found to be extremely profitable permanent companies were formed. Such companies were granted royal charters giving them the monopoly of trade with a specific area. Unlike the old regulated companies these associations were profit-making concerns, and non-members were not allowed to trade in their areas of influence. Consequently the individual merchant found it very difficult to compete. In the same manner the fair was pushed even further into the background, because the joint stock companies had no need of their facilities.

As the European nations strengthened their control over the new lands colonial empires came into being. At first Spain and Portugal had a virtual monopoly, and in 1494 the Pope divided Asia and America between them. Other maritime nations, England, France and Holland, began to claim a share in the New World. These colonies were jealously guarded as they were looked upon as a source of profit to the mother country. Only the powerful joint stock companies were influential enough to gain a share in this lucrative trade. A completely new form of trade had come into being. The colonies were used as a source of cheap raw materials, and a market for surplus manufactured goods. New products such as coffee, tea, cane-sugar and tobacco created industries. The need to produce manufactured goods suitable for the tropics led to a minor industrial revolution, as new methods and techniques had to be developed. Many of the older centres of industry and trade were unable to adapt to the new conditions, and more enterprising towns came to the forefront. Once again the link between the fair and commerce had been weakened.

The New World had another detrimental influence upon the fair. During the Middle Ages the shortage of gold and silver made the credit facilities available at the fair very important. With the Spanish conquest of South America, in the decades following 1520, large quantities of gold and the output of the Peruvian silver mines became available to the Spanish Crown. The wide responsibilities of the Emperor Charles V, who also ruled Spain, and the ambitious policies of his successor Philip II, meant that this wealth was soon diffused throughout Europe. The merchant classes were the first to benefit from the greater wealth, and many families began to loan out their surplus capital. Consequently nearly every town had its banking family, and the merchant, or farmer, no longer had to wait for the annual fair to obtain money for his yearly trading requirements.

The fair, which for centuries had been in the forefront of commerce, had become an anachronism. This did not mean, however, that it disappeared. Indeed the fairground was to have a very vigorous life for several centuries, an existence that is only now gradually coming to an end. The rôle of the fair underwent a radical change, which was a combination of increased local importance, and a return to a primarily social position. The cycle had come full turn, and the fair was once again to be a place of entertainment and revelry.

Epilogue

IT MUST not be thought that this change came overnight, because like most historical cycles, the change was very slow, with long periods of transition. The first important watershed came early in the sixteenth century with the coming of the English Reformation. When Henry VIII had completed his break away from the Roman Catholic Church, he turned his attention to the monastic houses, those last strongholds of Popery. Royal commissioners visited the monasteries, inevitably finding some fault, and by 1540 all the houses had been closed. The inmates were dispersed, and the alms-houses, schools and hospitals associated with them disappeared, or passed into lay hands. The same fate overtook many of the fairs, and certainly the link which had existed with the Church for a thousand years had come to an end. A good example of this type of change was Stourbridge Fair. In 1589 Elizabeth I transferred the fair charter to the town authorities, only allowing the Colleges to control the Weights and Measures, and the conduct of vagabonds and harlots on the fairground. The action of the Crown was not in any way intended as an attack upon the fairs, but was merely an outward sign of the assumption of ecclesiastical authority.

It was the beginning of an important alteration in the character of the fair, however, as the restraining influence of the Church was removed, and a greater atmosphere of worldliness began to creep into the fairground. Thereafter the fairs began to become less restrained, and rowdiness and frivolity increased rapidly. It is true that the medieval fair had a reputation for free-license, but many of the fairs became so licentious and unsavoury that respectable people would not visit them. It must be admitted, however, that this cannot be attributed entirely to the removal of ecclesiastical restraint, but to the growing importance of the fair-ground as a place of entertainment. Although the fairs certainly retained their importance in the country's economy, they had lost their international position, and this gap was filled with attractions of popular appeal.

The effect of this evolution was becoming apparent in the seventeenth century, a period when the national morality was not noted for its restraint. Many fairs continued to expand, and attracted even greater crowds than they had done in the Middle Ages. Wholesale trading continued to predominate, but now as an internal exchange between English industries. A noticeable change was the amount of retail dealing, aimed entirely at the casual visitors. Merchants had come to regard the fairs as a time to boost their normal sales, a holiday occasion when people were prepared to spend more money than at other times of the year. Another development was the marked increased in the number of stalls and booths devoted to the sale of cooked meats and other delicacies. The forms of entertainment had increased, and become more garish and sophisticated. The jousting, archery, and bull-baiting of the Middle Ages were no longer popular, and new wonders had to be found to whet the jaded tastes of the crowds.

The best example of the seventeenth century fair was in London, where St Bartholomew's was already acquiring the notoriety, that was to lead, eventually, to its closure. Although, like many fairs, it had suffered a temporary eclipse during the rule of Oliver Cromwell and the Commonwealth, when Puritan morality had forbidden all types of merrymaking, the fair was well re-established during the reign of Charles II. Samuel Pepys records his visits to Bartholomew Fair at a time when it was still permissible for people of good birth to be seen on the fairground: although even he regrets having to mix with so many 'nasty' people. Like so many of the crowd he went with no real intention of buying anything, but to walk round to see the sights, visit the side shows, and to take advantage of any pretty women in holiday mood. His attention was mainly taken with the fortune tellers, and puppet shows, or such attractions as monkeys dancing on ropes and horses with hooves like ram's horns. He was not particularly taken with the plays based upon scriptural stories, but found the grand spectacles very entertaining, if somewhat garish. These were based on allegorical, or classical themes, such as 'Neptune and Venus', with mermaids, dolphins and very colourful scenery. Such productions were based on the 'masque', which had been introduced into England from France, and had become very popular with the Court and the nobility. The day would be rounded off with the purchase of 'fairings', colourful ribbons and lace, or novelties, such as jewellery made of patterns of little glass balls. At this time Bartholomew Fair had grown so large that it extended into four parishes, and was a diversion for the nobility and courtiers.

By the eighteenth century England was beginning to undergo fundamental economic changes. The countryside was to be transformed by the building of the new turnpike roads, and the great open fields were disappearing with the growth of the enclosure movement so necessary for the improvement of farming. The population was expanding rapidly, and new towns were springing up in the north as the farm labourers began to drift from the land to factories of the Industrial Revolution. The position of the fair does not seem to have undergone any fundamental change. Daniel Defoe who made a tour of England at the beginning of the century leaves a very clear account of the fair at this time,[*] which does much to confirm the economic importance of the fair despite its increasing frivolity. On a visit to Bury St Edmunds in Suffolk Defoe commented: "It is true Bury Fair, like Bartholomew Fair, is a fair for diversion, more than for trade: and it may be a fair for toys and for trinkets, which the ladies may think fit to lay out some of their money in, as they see occasion. But to judge from thence, that the knights daughters of Norfolk, Cambridge-shire, and Suffolk, that is to say, for it cannot be understood any otherwise, the daughters of all the gentry of the three counties, come hither to be pick'd up, is a way of speaking I never before heard. . . . . .".[†] True Defoe was writing to refute a slander on the virtue of the East Anglian ladies, but it does give a good impression of the atmosphere of the fair at this period, and confirms that commerce was taking a secondary place at most fairgrounds.

It must not be thought, however, that all the fairs were given over to gaiety and vulgarity, and there was great local variation. Markets and fairs continued to perform an almost essential part in the distribution of certain food and commodities. The months of August and September saw the picture of 'droves' of turkeys and geese being driven from East Anglia to London and Stourbridge Fair. These flocks numbered from five hundred to two thousand birds being driven slowly along by young girls. The birds were specially bred for this particular time as it came immediately after harvest, and during their journey the geese could feed on the stubble along the way. By the beginning of October the roads were becoming too muddy for the birds to walk on and the traffic had to come to an end. The demand was becoming so great in

***

[*]Daniel Defoe, *A Tour Through the Whole Island of Great Britain*, Vol. 1, Everyman's Library.
[†]*Op. cit.* Page 51.

London, however, that a new type of cart was invented with four storeys, one above the other to carry the geese and turkeys. It was pulled by two horses harnessed abreast, instead of in tandem as was usual with carts. By this means the birds could be carried nearly a hundred miles in two days and a night.

Another unmistakable sign of the continuing economic vitality of the fair, was the Yarmouth Herring Fair. It must be remembered that the luxury of being able to buy fresh fish is a comparatively recent development. Until the nineteenth century most people living any distance from the sea had to eat fresh water fish, because it was impossible to transport fresh sea fish quickly enough. This is the reason why all the monasteries had their own stews, or fish ponds. Most of our important fishing ports were then obscure villages, the exception to this was the port of Great Yarmouth. Here apart from a very vigorous overseas trade, herrings played a very important part. Every year on Michaelmas Day the Herring Fair was held, at the time when the herring shoals appeared off the East Anglian coast, and lasted for the whole month of October, until the shoals left for deeper waters to spawn. The entire shoreline was lined with the curing sheds, where the herrings were smoked, and then sealed in barrels. Merchants from all over the country came to Yarmouth to buy the fish, and up to 40,000 barrels could be sold during the fair. This was quite apart from the normal supplies to the neighbouring towns, and the barrels exported to the Mediterranean countries.

No description of the fair in the eighteenth century would be complete without Stourbridge Fair. Although it must be remembered that Stourbridge was the last of the great English fairs, and was in many ways unique. Indeed Defoe writes: "I came necessarily through Sturbridge Fair. . . . . which is not only the greatest in the whole nation, but in the world; nor, if I may believe those who have seen them all, is the fair at Leipsick in Saxony, the mart at Frankfort on the Main, or the fairs at Neuremberg, or Augsburg, any way to compare to this fair at Sturbridge.* The fair continued to be held on its traditional site, a large cornfield of approximately half a square mile, near the village of Casterton. The farmers tilling the land had to have their crops harvested by the beginning of September, otherwise the fair people were allowed to walk over the crops to set up their booths. These were set up in long streets

*Op. cit. Page 80.

94

around a central square. The streets themselves had names, such as Cheapside, which was where every type of London retail trader could be found. The other rows were mainly wholesale, but there was a large number of retail merchants. The square, or Duddery, measured 100 yards by 80 yards, and was used for unloading by the wholesale cloth dealers, whose booths surrounded it. The early stages of the fair was devoted to the sale of cloth, and there was a tremendous turnover: up to £100,000 worth of business being completed within the week. ". . . . by wholesalemen, from London, and all other parts of England, who transact their business wholly in their pocket books, and meeting their chapmen from all parts, making up their accounts, receiving money chiefly in bills, and taking orders."* The extent of the wealth of cloth on display can be gauged from the fact that in one booth owned by a Norwich 'stuff' merchant alone there was £20,000 worth of materials. It was not only the East Anglian clothiers who predominated at Stourbridge but large numbers came from the West Country. Already the manufacturers in Yorkshire were beginning to expand, as was the cotton industry in Lancashire. A sign of this was the thousands of packhorses, which came to Stourbridge from Manchester and the north.

Despite the abundance of cloth sold a greater part of the turnover of orders was taken by the merchants. Defoe estimates that each cloth wholesaler went away with £10,000 worth of orders. This applied equally to the manufacturers of heavy materials, such as the braziers and iron-masters, or the wine merchants. The reason for this was the difficulty and expense of transporting heavy goods. One of the great advantages of Stourbridge was that all the bulky merchandise could be brought to the fairground by water, as the river Cam formed one boundary to the site. Cloth was sent from Norwich and the other weaving centres in East Anglia along the rivers Waveney and Stour to the Ouse and thence to Stourbridge. Merchandise from all other parts of the country was sent by ship to the port of Lynn, where it could be transhipped to barges for carriage along the Ouse. It was this facility which made Stourbridge so popular and long lasting. Once the bulk of the cloth sales were over, the second part of the fair was devoted mainly to the sale of wool and hops. This part of the fair was particularly important for the Norwich manufacturers, because the wool from East Anglian

---

*Ibid. Page 81.

sheep was not well suited to the making of a high quality worsted cloth. A large proportion of the wool on sale at Stourbridge came from Leicestershire, and was of the long staple variety needed for worsted manufacture. Although the quantities sold did not equal the total of cloth, it was still considerable, amounting to some £60,000 worth. To some extent the sale of hops was even more important than either cloth, or wool. The reason for this was that the main hop growing areas in southern England were Kent, Surrey, and the Chelmsford area of Essex, and the bulk of the crop was sent to Stourbridge. The prices set at the fair set the national prices for the whole country. As very few hops were grown in the north of England all the brewers from those parts had to come to Stourbridge for their supplies, as did the brewers of the Midlands and East Anglia.

Cambridge was the main centre for accommodation, but the crowds were so vast that there was not nearly enough room for them all. Every town and village for a wide radius were so crammed that the local farmers were able to rent out their barns, stables and sheds at a very good profit. The fair people themselves, except for the wealthy merchants, slept in their booths, and as there was such an abundance of cookshops and other food booths, there was never any shortage of supplies on the fairground. Some idea of the press of people hurrying to and from the fairground is given by the fact that London dealers were prepared to send fifty hackney carriages to Stourbridge to carry people from Cambridge alone. At the same time other Londoners considered it worth while to send Thames wherries all the way to Cambridge on carts to ply for trade along the river Cam. Surprisingly, in view of the rowdiness and bad reputations gained by many eighteenth century fairs, Defoe comments that he had never seen such a large crowd so well behaved.

Once the serious business of the fair had been completed, the last few days were given over to more entertainment. This was the time when the local gentry from all the neighbouring counties came to Stourbridge in order to see the sights, and to buy trinkets and novelties from the stalls. At this time greater emphasis was put on the puppet and side shows, which included a variety of 'drolls', both human and animal. One of the great attractions for the gentry was that the closing day was devoted to a horse fair, at which they were able to replenish their stables at lower prices than at Tattersalls. To entertain the meaner section of the crowd a number of horse and foot races were provided. On this festive note the fair came to an end, and the fairground was rapidly cleared: the dung, straw and rubbish being left for the farmers to plough in to manure their strips for the following year.

By the beginning of the next century the Industrial Revolution was well established, and the industrial strength of England had shifted from south-eastern counties to the north. The new industrial complexities had little need of the fairs for the marketing of their goods and so the turnover of trade at Stourbridge began to dwindle. There was no such slackening of trade at fairs such as Bartholomew's which catered primarily for entertainment. At the time when the battle of Waterloo was being fought Bartholomew Fair was continuing to attract huge crowds. The type of entertainment being offered had begun to undergo yet another change. The puppet shows were still a great attraction, as were Mr Simon Paap the Celebrated Dutch Dwarf and the other drolls. The nineteenth century love of the grotesque and melodramatic was becoming more apparent. In Richardson's Great Booth plays such as the 'Hall of Death, or Who's the Murderer,' were horrific enough to please the most exacting fairgoer. Other certain successes were the 'Learned Pig', the 'Living Skeleton', and the 'Fireproof Lady', who dipped her hands into boiling oil. A sign of the growth of industrialism was the appearance of animated and clockwork toys. These usually took the form of dolls which were operated by strings attached to the operator's foot, and were animated to dance in time to music. By this time these were becoming more elaborate with the dolls being worked by clockwork. The vulgarity and licentiousness of the fair had become so pronounced, that no one with any pretentions of good reputation and birth could be seen on the fairground, which was given over to the lower classes, apart from the young society 'bloods', and 'ladies' of doubtful reputation.

It was at this time, 1814, that the last of the great London Frost Fairs was held. These were rare occurrences because they were held on the ice when the river Thames froze hard enough to support the weight of the booths and people. Such fairs were devoted entirely to entertainment, although enterprising shopkeepers were quick to take advantage of the trade offered. The first recorded Frost Fair was in 1554, and the other main occasions were in 1684, 1715 and 1739. These fairs were possible at this time because England underwent a little ice age from the thirteenth to the nineteenth century, when the climate deteriorated to such an extent that the once important grape farming in southern England came to an end. By the nineteenth century the temperature had begun to rise slightly. This was hastened by the Industrial Revolution, the vast quantities of smoke and carbon dioxide belched out by the factories creating an industrial haze, which prevented heavy frosts. The demolition of old London Bridge, with its many piers, in 1825, completely precluded the possibility of further frost fairs, by speeding the flow of the Thames and making it less liable to freezing.

Another event in 1825, the opening of the Stockton to Darlington Railway, presaged another vital threat to the fair. Despite great opposition, a network of railway lines was rapidly established in Britain, providing fast and cheap transport for heavy goods. This struck a final blow to the commercial usefulness of the fair and one of the first to disappear was the Yarmouth Herring Fair. Fresh sea fish packed in ice could now be distributed rapidly by railway to the towns, and the fair was no longer needed even in times of glut. The coming of the railways made it possible to carry livestock much more easily, and this again had an adverse effect upon the animal sales at the fairs, which had remained important when other transactions had fallen off. If anything the railways were beneficial to the purely entertainment fairs. Bartholomew Fair was still flourishing, and in 1839 the rent for the booths was doubled. Yet within sixteen years both Bartholomew and Stourbridge Fairs had come to an end, swept away in the welter of municipal and social legislation of the middle decades of the century. Most of the fairs continued, but in a very much reduced scale, and without any rights of jurisdiction. St Ives Fair, for instance, did not disappear, but only lasted for one day on Whit Monday. Even so the coming of the steam age was a great boon to the fairs, which were now purely places for amusement. Steam engines and organs became the central features of the fairground, providing music, roundabouts, and funfares.

In its new guise the fair continued to hold its popularity until the twentieth century. Until after the First World War the Mop Fairs continued to be important for the hiring of domestic servants, and, indeed, in some areas there were Runaway Mop Fairs held a few weeks later, where servants, dissatisfied with their choice of employment, could offer themselves to new masters. By the 1920s the size of households began to decline, and the number of house servants required grew less. In any case there was a growing feeling of equality, which made people less willing to work as servants. By the thirties other forms of entertainment were beginning to offer rival forms of amusement. The bicycle and the motor car were becoming a popular form of recreation. These, however, only involved a relatively small number of people and of much wider appeal were the wireless and the cinema, which were beginning to gather large audiences. Another invention of this time, which was to have a much greater influence upon the fair, was television. It was not until the decades after the Second World War that television sets became cheap enough to have a popular appeal. By the 1950s television was entertaining mass audiences; the number of people attending the fairs declined still further.

Today the fair can still be seen on the village green, but is finding it difficult to compete with the range of sophisticated amusements available on every hand. Gone is the day when the fair was the main event of the year. Now it is just one more diversion among many others, and so has returned to the obscurity out of which it sprang.

Appendix

*A Step to Stir-Bitch Fair**

For another and more rumbustious account of Stourbridge Fair the reader should turn to an account written in the year 1700 by a Mr E. Ward. Although it conveys much the same information as the more sedate description given by Defoe, *A Step to Stir-Bitch Fair* conveys a better impression of the debauchery of an eighteenth century fair. It soon become apparent why no woman with the slightest pretention of respectability could afford to be seen on a fairground.

The title itself quickly establishes the attitude of many of the visitors to the fairground, most of whom certainly did not come for the more mundane merchandise. It is equally clear that many of the merchants themselves had thoughts beyond dealings in their normal stock in trade:— "Their pretence is, coming down to meet their customers; tho' its plain by their Loitering, they have little else to do but to Drink, Smoke, and Whore, and to help support the Fair in its Ancient Custom of Debauchery." The author's lengthy account of the journey from London to Cambridge supports the view that a visit to the fair was an excuse for many to enjoy themselves as much as possible as a consolation for the temporary parting from their wives. Behind the facade of respectability almost everything to do with the fair seems to have catered for the requirements of the single man.

The presence of such a large number of London hackney carriages is made more understandable. It is true that for a fare of 3d. a head the drivers were prepared to fill their carriages full to overflowing with the "Tag, Rag, and Bobtail" wishing to go to the fairground. This was not the most lucrative branch of their trade, which seems to have been the gentle art of procuring. For a fare of 1s. 6d. the carriage could be turned into "a running Bawdy-house", sheltered from curious eyes by tin shutters. Between Cambridge and the fairground was the village of Barnwell which seems to have

---

A Step to Stir-Bitch Fair, E. Ward 1700. (By courtesy of the Cambridge Collection, Cambridge Libraries).

acquired the somewhat unenviable title of "Bawdy-Barnwell". Traditionally the village was supposed to provide recreation for the Cambridge students, although the townspeople were not so readily welcomed. This close relationship dated back to the reign of Henry I, when the University came into being, whereafter it was reputed to be impossible to find a virgin in Barnwell over the age of sixteen. For the non-academic there was plenty of alternative entertainment to be found on the actual fairground: there being an abundance of, "Ladies . . . . . being as commendable for their good nature, as remarkable for their prettiness."

One custom remarkable to Stourbridge was the 'christening' of Freshmen. Newcomers were lured by their friends into an empty booth where the presiding diety of Stourbridge, "Lord Tap", recited the following verse:

> Over thy Head I ring this Bell,
> Because thou art an Infidel;
> And I have found thee out by th' Smell:
> With a Hoxius Doxius call upon him,
> That no Vengeance may Light on him.

The recipient was then given a bawdy name bestowed by his two 'godfathers'. He. was expected to pay a fine of 5s. for the entertainment of the christening party, and then he was free of the seamier side of fairground life.

SUGGESTIONS FOR FURTHER READING

Balison M., *Borough Customs,* Selden Society.

Beaumont A., *Fair Organs,* Model and Allied Publications.

Beaumont A., *Traction Engines on Parade,* Model and Allied Publications.

Braithwaite D., *Fairground Architecture,* Evelyn.

Broome D., *Fairground Billy,* Brockhampton.

Chambers E. K., *The Medieval Stage,* 1903.

Craig H., *English Religious Drama of the Middle Ages,* Oxford University Press.

Fuller J., *Fairground Music,* Chatto.

Geddes N., *Fairs,* Matter of Fact Books, Methuen.

Gassner J., ed., *Drama Medieval and Tudor,* Baiton Books.

Grant M., *The Fair,* Grosseteste.

Green J. R., *Town Life in the Fifteenth Century,* 1894.

Groves P and Stratta L., *The Fair,* Longman.

Harbage A., *Annals of English Drama 975-1700,* Methuen.

Matthews R. C. O., *Study in Trade-Cycle History,* Cambs.

Moss P., *Sports and Pastimes through the Ages,* Harrap.

Pease G. H. and Chitty H., ed. Parrish H., *Law of Markets and Fairs,* Knight.

Richardson H., *Fairs and Markets of York,* Anthony's Press, York.

Rossiter A. P., *English Drama from Early Times to the Elizabethans.*

Salzman L. F., *Trade in the Middle Ages,* Oxford University Press.

Toulmin-Smith L., *English Gilds,* Early English Text Society.

Toulmin-Smith L., *The York Mystery Plays,* 1885.

Unwin G. *Studies in Economic History,* 1927.

Wilkins F., *Fairs,* Learning Library, Blackwell.

Wilson D. R., *Roman Frontiers of Britain,* Heinemann Educational.

Wilson F. P., *English Drama 1485-1585,* Oxford Histories.

PLAN OF STIRBITCH OR STOURBRI[DGE]

A — Blackmore Head
B — Black Swan
C — Booksellers Row
D — Braziers Row
E — Brush Row
F — Cheapside Row
G — Cheese Row
H — Coffee Booth
J — (Sir John) Cotton's
K — (Mr) Finch
L — Fish Hill
M — Greave's Booth
N — (Mr) Jenning's House
O — Joyner's Row
P — Leather Fair
Q — Market Place
R — Marshalls Booth
S — Music Booth
T — Oyster Fair
U — Paper Mills and Damm
    Close
V — Proctors House
W — Servants
X — Show Booths
Y — (Mr) Skiner's House
Z — Soap Hill
a — Soapers Row
b — Tallow Hill
c — Trunk Row
d — Turners Row
e — Upwoods Booth
f — White Hart
g — White Leather Fair

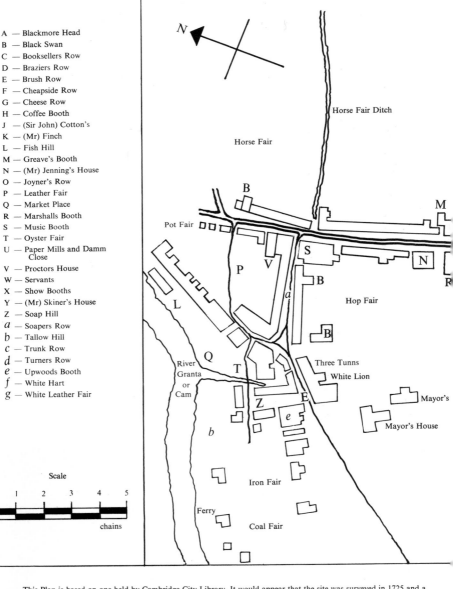

Scale

0   1   2   3   4   5

chains

This Plan is based on one held by Cambridge City Library. It would appear that the site was surveyed in 1725 and a plan was kept in Mayor's House 'in Stirbitch Field'. In October, 1775 Mr Freeman, a Painter of Cambridge, made a copy for which he charged one guinea. In November, 1816 James Tall of Cambridge took a copy of Mr Freeman's plan and this was presented to the Cambridge Free Library, by Mr Henry Wallis, in 1887. This map also gives the following information "For the right ascertaining the several parts of Sturebridge Fair, there are stones that lay under the Ploughshare as marked as to show the several Divisions—these stones are called Dole Stones" "No Proprietor of Booth- Grounds has a Right to build *deeper than 14ft*—all behind or before belongs to the Baliffs Waste and is let from 4 pence to 6 pence and 12 pence per foot". "The Cheesemongers are allowed 6 *feet in front and 6 feet behind*